DEVELOPING CHARACTER FOR CLASSROOM SUCCESS

Strategies to Increase Responsibility, Achievement, and Motivation in Secondary Students

Charlie Abourjilie
High School Teacher and Coach

CHARACTER
DEVELOPMENT
PUBLISHING

D1550724

For information, contact:
Character Development Publishing
P.O. Box 9211
Chapel Hill NC 27515-9211
(919) 967-2110, fax (919) 967-2139
E-mail: respect96@aol.com
www.CharacterEducation.com

Cover and text design by Sara Sanders
Text editing by Ginny Turner

ISBN 1-892056-07-0

$12.00

Quantity Purchases
Companies, schools, professional groups, clubs, and other organizations may qualify for special terms when ordering quantities of this title. For ordering information, contact the Customer Service Department of Character Development Publishing at the numbers listed above.

2nd Printing 2002

*For all of my students
and everyone lucky enough
to be called teacher or coach*

"A teacher affects eternity; he can never tell where his influence stops."
—Henry Adams

"I am a teacher. A teacher is someone who leads. There is no magic here. I do not walk on water. I do not part the sea. I just love the children."
—Marva Collins

Table of Contents

Foreword by Dr. Philip Fitch Vincent 1

Thank You 3

Introduction. 7

Author's Note 11

Chapter 1 13
A Classroom Teacher's Definition of "Character Education"

Chapter 2 17
What's This Guy Up To?

Chapter 3 23
Guiding Principles

Chapter 4 33
Techniques and Practices for the Classroom

Closing Thoughts 81

Afterword: Ten More Reasons for Character Education 83

Appendix: Multicultural Golden Rule 89

Bibliography & Suggested Readings 91

About the Author 93

Foreword

Charlie Abourjilie reminds me of my educational hero, Hobart Cook. Mr. Cook taught algebra and chemistry in the late 1960s at Cummings High School in Burlington, North Carolina. I remember very little about the content of the chemistry or algebra classes, but I remember clearly how Mr. Cook taught. He modeled how we were to treat each other, teaching us by his example, not just his words. Despite his expectations that we work hard, every one of us knew that Mr. Cook cared for us. He also expected us to be respectful and responsible. We were held accountable for our actions, and we earned our grades. There were very few failures, either socially or academically. Mr. Cook taught academics and character, but thirty years later, what I remember are his lessons on character.

This is how Charlie views education—as a great opportunity to develop young people into adults we can admire and trust. His students love him, but not because he's a softie who throws high grades at them for showing up. They like the way he sets limits and expects them to be respectful and to perform to the best of their ability. He assumes they will, and they generally do. Their resulting academic accomplishments in his class fuel their self-respect in other areas of their life. They also forge strong bonds with Charlie, who truly has never met a kid he didn't love and care about. Charlie is the high school teacher you pray your child will get.

Teachers who are successful in connecting with their students and earning their respect and admiration find it easy to get their curriculum content across. They motivate students to learn because they themselves are excited about helping students learn. You may know your material inside out, but if you don't care about your students, or if you lack interest in the wonderful process of teaching and learning, your effectiveness as a teacher will be seriously diminished.

In your hand, you hold a treasure box of ideas from one of our most successful classroom teachers, who offers his road-tested techniques for keeping students interested and participating in their own education. It's also an expression of Charlie's joyful teaching philosophy, which I hope will infuse you with new spark and desire for the adventure of teaching. Charlie has had batches of tough, tough students, and he's experienced all the frustration of teaching, but he still considers his days on his feet in the classroom to be deeply satisfying.

You will find good ideas and creative teaching techniques in Charlie's book. Try the ones you like right away. Both you and your students will absorb valuable lessons about learning and life, and you're likely to find you enjoy your work more. When that happens, thank Charlie.

—Dr. Philip Fitch Vincent

Thank You

Writing a book over a one-year-plus period takes a lot more determination and inspiration than one man, especially I, can generally muster. I never thought I'd write a book, and I'm still far from what I consider an author. Finding the words to put down took inspiration and support from many people. I would like to give them the credit and thank them for what they have contributed to this endeavor, my teaching, and ultimately my life. I have been blessed by their presence in my life. I am deeply grateful to count them as my family and friends. To all of the following people, I say a heartfelt **THANK YOU!**

My mom and dad are my heroes. They have given me everything in the world and taught me so much through their words and actions—love, patience, caring, understanding, and never-ending support. My mom passed away due to cancer in 1993, but I have never been without her. I talk to her and think about her every single day. She is the greatest person I have ever known. Mom and her example are my source of strength. My father is not only the best father in the world, but he was also the best husband. His love and dedication to my mother showed me what being a real man is all about—love, kindness, caring, and giving. When I grow up I want to be just like my mom and dad. My mom and dad raised three pretty good kids. I love my sisters, **Becky** and **Denise**, dearly. They have always been there for me.

My wife, **Karen, and children, Jordan, Cole, and Austin,** are the center of my life. Being a husband and father is the greatest, most exciting and thrilling thing in the world. It isn't easy, but nothing worthwhile is easy. I laugh and cry daily with my family. I would have nothing without my family. **Karen** is my reality check, encourager, and friend. She helps keep me somewhat pointed in the right direction. My daughter, **Jordan,** has been a particularly bright inspiration during the writing of this book. She was always asking how it's coming and asking if I'm done yet. She always wants to read what I've been working on. She is my little princess. **Cole** is my energy boost. His smile and wink could light up the darkest, deepest cave. He is a sweet, sweet boy who loves his family. Our new baby, **Austin,** is a joy and is as beautiful as our other two. I have been blessed beyond belief.

Friends help us define life and who we are. As I was growing up and as an adult, I've had some of the greatest friends in the world. I'm proud and very fortunate to say that the close group of friends I had through high school is still close today. We called ourselves the **HAWDs—Richard, Sean, Matt, Steve L., Steve K.,** and me. We did everything together then and still keep in touch today, though we all live several hundred miles apart. Whenever any of us get together, it's like we've never been separated.

Todd and **Doug** were my two roommates for three years at Virginia Tech. We went through so much and enjoyed so much together, it's like a storybook friendship. We were so lucky to find each other as roommates—it's like we were brothers. My memories of those days still bring a smile to my face and a deep laugh from within. **Stewart, John, Kirk, Lamont, and Larry, and all the folks at Bear Island**—they taught me that you can work hard, have fun, and build great relationships with people regardless of their differences. All of these guys are the greatest.

My friends/teachers I've taught with over the past ten+ years have shaped me and my teaching more than words can describe. They have helped me to grow as both a teacher and person. These folks are my peers, my role models, great teachers, and wonderful people I also call "friends": **Terri Green, Annette Greene, Becky Yaun, Joanne Morgan, Richard Welch, Cheryl Southern, Sylvia Smith, Karen Abourjilie** (my wife), and **Bobbie Cobb**. Two of my very closest friends and two of the finest people, teachers, and coaches in the world are **Jim Coggins** and **Donna Christy. Laverne Bass**, an assistant principal at our school several years ago, was one of the greatest administrators I've ever had the opportunity to work and learn under. Not only is Ms. Bass a true instructional leader, but she was also the "caring leader" of our school. Superior young teachers like **Tracy Repko, Meghan McGlinn, and Esa Cox** motivate me by their contagious enthusiasm and commitment. I have been blessed to know and work with these people and all of the people at Southwest Guilford High School. I have learned a lot from so many there—the custodial staff, secretaries, media specialists, our counselors, and all of our teachers. I am indebted to them all.

Great educators, such as **Harry Wong, Marva Collins, Clare Lemeres, Carl Boyd, Larry Bell, Hal Urban, Tom Lickona, Helen LeGette, David Brooks, James O'Brian, Jerry Graham, Mel Swann, Lillie Jones, James Ingram, Harry Dent, Ben Nesbit, Lynn Macan, and Larry Allred** have taught me so much through their leadership, teachings, and examples. I doubt these people really know what amazing effects they have on the lives they touch. Our profession owes them a great deal.

This book would never have been possible without the tremendous efforts and support of two close friends, **Phil Vincent** and **Deb Brown**. Their encouragement and suggestions were priceless. The help and dedication of **Dixon Smith**, and **Ginny Turner**, my editor, at Character Development Publishing, made this book a reality. Ginny revised my attempt at writing into a work worth reading. I can't thank them enough.

And last, but not least, I thank **my students**. Without them, I wouldn't be here. They've been a daily source of inspiration, laughter, warmth, and encouragement. What's really neat is that my kids already know how I feel about them—that I care about and love them. You know how you sometimes have a special class or group you get close to? Well, I've had more than fifty of them. They've shown me that even when kids are 14 to 18 years old and look all grown up, they aren't. They've shown me how much difference I can make in their lives, but they don't realize how much difference they've made in mine.

> "Without struggle there can be no progress."
>
> —Frederick Douglass

Introduction

"Charlie, what do you think about being a fireman, or working for the cable company—that appears to be a growing business."

Those were the words of my high school counselor my senior year. The message I heard was, "You aren't college material" and "You aren't smart enough." That conversation did not move me to great changes for my life that day, but it was definitely stored away in my memory. Mrs. Mayfield probably had good reason to make that statement. I had never given her reason to think that I was particularly scholarly. I just had never given great thought to what I wanted to do with my future. To quote Phil Vincent, "I was severely, profoundly average." Mom always wanted me to be a preacher, and dad liked the idea of his son being a dentist. Me, I was just happy going to school with my friends, playing sports, and trying to get a date. Who wanted to think about a future career? My future consisted of the weekend and summer break! Being a teacher was the last thing I'd have had in mind.

Now, seventeen years later, I am just that—a teacher and coach. I've been in the classroom for over ten years and still love it. I teach great kids the subject of social studies in a public high school that serves approximately 1,200 students. That's not too large, but considering the school was built for around 800, it gets a little tight. I also spent ten years coaching football and women's basketball. I always bring up the coaching because it has meant so much to me and has helped make me the teacher I am. Even though I don't now coach, some kids still call me "Coach Abo." They came up with it because Abourjilie (A-ber-jay-lee) was too difficult to say quickly.

The kids I teach are some of the greatest in the world. My favorite subjects to teach are U.S. history, government, and current events. Those are the subjects I'm teaching this year, all on the college preparatory level (out of CP, Honors, and AP). I have also taught the higher levels of those classes, and psychology as well. The kids in my classes have come in all shapes, sizes, colors, and ability levels. A sampling of the labels I've seen include BEH, LD, OHI, ADD, ADHD, Willie M, EMH, TMH, At-risk, and AG. That's over ten years, but also would apply to my first period class from last year—a class with 39 students. This may sound tough, but I don't think it's anything that any classroom teacher in a public school hasn't faced. We all face it every day.

So, how did this teacher and coach come to write a book? That was my thinking as well. "I'm just a teacher and coach," I said flippantly, as if it was no big deal, but I was wrong. Being a teacher is the second toughest and greatest job in the world, second only to being a parent. Five days a week I have the chance to make a difference in the lives of 140+ children. A difference that may last the period, the day, or a lifetime.

In 1994 I attended a workshop about motivation, responsibility, and achievement for at-risk children. It was presented by a woman from California named Clare Lemeres. She was wonderful. She gave me many great ideas, but more than anything she inspired me to share my new enthusiasm with others. I went back to my school the next day and told my principal how great the training was that I'd been to, and asked him if I could present it to our staff later that year. He said yes, and that is how I got started presenting.

Over the years I have been tremendously impressed with the work and philosophical principles of Harry Wong and Marva Collins. I've combined their material along with that of many wonderful teachers and coaches I've worked with over the years, and have tried to share this with as many colleagues as possible. I readily followed Harry Wong's advice to "beg, borrow, and steal" tips and ideas from great teachers. Soon I was presenting at different schools and conferences around the state. In the last two years I have been blessed by getting to hear and meet such wonderful educators as Tom Lickona, Phil Vincent, Kevin Ryan, Harry Dent, Deb Brown, David Brooks, and Hal Urban—all working with character education. These inspiring professionals have helped me to be a better teacher.

I love teaching. I love my students, past and present. They have also been a great inspiration. I'm sure that I've learned as much from them as they have from me. This love for my profession and my students brings me great joy and satisfaction, and I want to help other teachers find ways to experience these deep, happy feelings. Teaching should not be a job that people dread going to, or one that people regret entering—and it doesn't have to be. I have fun teaching. I have fun with my students. My kids are able to pick me up when I'm down. I think it should and could be like that for every teacher.

Don't I get tired? Yep. Don't my legs hurt sometimes after standing and walking around the class all day? Yep, and even more so after coaching for an additional two to four hours. Don't I get frustrated with my kids? Yep, sometimes. Sometimes I will do the morning announcements at my school, and on Monday morning I'll say, "T.G.I.M." and tell the student body how excited I am to have them there and how excited I am about their opportunity to learn that week. Then on Friday, I'll say, "T.G.I.F." and tell them how excited I am to have a couple days away from them and from grading papers. They know I love them and can't wait to see them on Monday, but they also know I'm ready for a break on Friday, just as they are. Teaching is not an easy job. Often it is downright difficult, but I've always told my classes and teams that nothing worthwhile is easy. Frederick Douglass said, "Without struggle, there can be no progress." That holds true for teaching, but I think it's the greatest job in the world, and there's nothing else I'd rather be doing.

I recently took a half-time position as what our system calls a Teacher On Special Assignment, or TOSA, working with character education. My new position calls for me to help the school system begin the character education process (something I will touch on later). Accepting this new position and opportunity meant I would have to leave two of my classes. This was a tough decision for me, and I prayed about it for a long time. I am very close to many of the kids I left. They are all super. After telling them of my plans, that I would be leaving fifth and sixth periods, and that they would be getting a new teacher, a young woman named "Phayth" came up to me and told me she was really sad to see me go. I had only known Phayth for a couple of months, while I'd known many of the kids for years, so I asked her why she was so sad. Phayth said, "Because you are the only teacher I have ever had that I felt liked every student in the class." Right then I realized why I was leaving. It shouldn't be like that. Phayth is sixteen years old, and she should have had dozens of teachers who gave her that feeling. That's why I'm writing this book. I want to share what I've learned and some things I do that I've taken from great teachers. I want all teachers to love their job and their kids as much as I do.

Author's Note

Developing *Character for Classroom Success* is meant to be a book about useful techniques for the secondary, or any, classroom that directly reflect the heart of character education—caring, responsibility, respect, honesty, achievement, and teacher role modeling. The techniques and activities described in this book come from teachers and educators I have worked with, heard, or read over the last eleven years. Much of it I have gotten from other teachers, though I use it or have used it all in my classroom. Some of it may not be new to you, but as Mark Twain said, "No one is smart enough to remember everything he knows." I also include some of the philosophies that guide my teaching. I hope this will give you some valuable ideas to use in your classroom and share with your kids, or be a reminder of things you've not used in a while. Good luck with these ideas and your students!

NOTE: My position, Teacher On Special Assignment as Character Education Coordinator, has been made full-time. I will serve in this capacity for two years, attempting to lead all of the schools in Guilford County to character education. This is a great mission, to build the character education process within an entire district (96 schools with 62,000+ students) and community—but I miss my classroom and students greatly. Once I get our schools off to a good start and help create a living vision, I will return to the classroom. This is a true learning experience, working with teachers, schools, and children K-12. I am fortunate to work in a system that so strongly supports this mission. I will return to the classroom at the start of the 2000-2001 school year...and can't wait!

CHAPTER 1

A Classroom Teacher's Definition of "Character Education"

"Education is not enough. Intelligence plus character—that is the true goal of education."

—Dr. Martin Luther King, Jr.

Character education is far more than the "flavor of the month" or an add-on program for any teacher. Actually, I think "character education" is a label recently placed on what is considered the essence of true, quality teaching. It has been present in America since 1607, and in the world since the beginning of time. Character education is caring about your students and teaching so we can help improve or advance the lives of the children we teach. It's really why anyone in education got into education—for children. It is not a program that you can take out of a box or place on a wall. It is the way we live our lives in front of our children.

In trying to best explain to groups of teachers, parents, school staffs, or community leaders what character education is, I always tell them that, in a nutshell, character education is "where the rubber meets the road" in education. By that I mean character education is about more than textbooks, standardized tests, and an overpacked curriculum. It is about preparing children for success—success in school, at work, in personal relationships, IN LIFE. The following story about a former student states it perfectly.

Last June our seniors graduated on a Friday night. It was a wonderful night of pride, excitement, and accomplishment. These young men and women had just completed thirteen years of school. They had met all the requirements and passed all the tests. Graduation nights are always full of exhilaration and joy. It was the same for all of our kids. On Monday morning, just three days later, I went to school to start breaking my room down, finish averaging year-end grades—all the stuff we do on that first workday after the kids are gone. As soon as I walked into the office to sign in, Dorothy Harrington, our guidance secretary, came up to me and, in a worried voice, said, "Coach Abo, did you hear about Steve?" I knew there hadn't been a fatal drunk-driving accident—I would have heard about that. When I told Dorothy I hadn't heard anything, she told me Steve had been arrested the night before, Sunday, for selling crack cocaine in a nearby neighborhood. He'd had a huge quantity and was being charged on several felony counts.

"Steve" had been a basketball star since seventh grade. He was a frequent starting point guard, had a great smile, had passed all the tests and requirements for graduation. Steve had plans of playing junior college basketball for two years, then planned on transferring to a division one school to play. He seemingly had it all—and he threw it all away. But that's not where the story ends. Later that summer the state released the latest accountability scores and ratings for high schools. My school was rated "Exemplary." I was excited and proud for about two seconds, then my thoughts went back to Steve. We didn't do an exemplary job with Steve. What had we taught him? Whatever it was, he sure didn't use it when the big test came—the test of life. Somewhere along the line someone dropped the ball. Actually, I think all of us—Steve, his teachers and coaches, his administrators, college recruiters, his counselors, his mom—all of us had fumbled the ball somewhere. I don't know if we did a good enough job teaching Steve how to make right choices, even when it was tough. To me that's what character education is about. Helping students to know how best to live their lives and to face the challenges of the world they will soon be immersed in. That's what I mean when I say it's where the rubber meets the road in education.

As I proudly tell groups when I'm speaking, I did not get into teaching to be the Educational Testing Service. I wanted to help change or influence students' lives in a positive way. My students do well on all the required state tests. The students' self-discipline in my room is strong. I can count on one hand the number of children I've had to send to the office or write up in the last ten years. It's not magic. I'm not a patsy who lets my kids get away with anything and everything—in fact it's just the opposite. From day one, my students know the expectations and limits that are placed on them. I waver little on principle, and I don't lower my high expectations. We get to know each other and what we are there for every day—to learn, have fun and explore together, and to become people of good character.

Character education must extend beyond the doors of the class-room. As a teacher of character, I need to be involved with my students' other teachers, their coaches, and their families. To be the best that I can be, I need to be aware of what's going on in the lives of my students. When I do these things, it makes my life as a classroom teacher much easier. With very few discipline problems, high expectations for learning and fun (because I think learning and discovering new things are fun), and an involved and caring class, I have more time to teach and a great atmosphere to teach in. I believe this focus on children, building relationships, and high expectations are why I love my profession more today than I did a decade ago.

Character education is not an add-on program. Sure, it *can* be if you go out and buy a new boxed curriculum and try to add it to your current curriculum. In my view, character education is what we do every day. It's how we greet, react to, and teach our children. If you say you don't teach character, you are wrong. The messages you send to your children through your classroom behavior, through your expectations, through your interactions with your students and their parents outside the classroom, all convey character education. It's in all the little things we do. We are all already character educators. The question is, what type of character are we teaching and modeling?

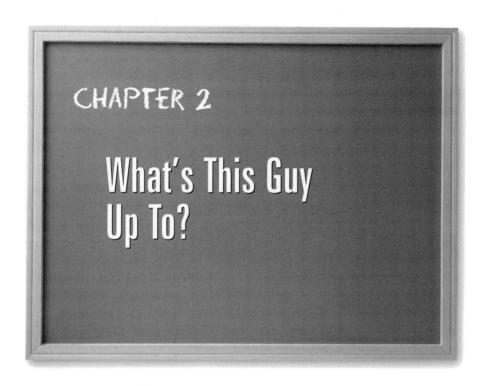

CHAPTER 2

What's This Guy Up To?

"Somebody needs you!"

—Larry Bell

Last year I was listening to a friend named Larry Bell speak about cultural diversity and minority student achievement. Larry has been a high school teacher and coach, and the Director of Cultural Diversity in Prince William County, Virginia. Now he's the CEO of his own business, Multicultural America. Larry is a dynamic speaker, and he started off talking about his "agenda." He said that it seemed like everyone had one these days, and so did he. Larry has served as a mentor for me in this new character education position, and knowing that I would be speaking to groups, I figured if Larry's got an agenda, I should have one too. I'm weary of the term "agenda" so I'll call it my "mission statement." My mission is simply this:

Encourage EVERYONE in a school to WANT to work TOGETHER to CHANGE children's lives POSITIVELY!

EVERYONE

Just as true character education involves all adults in the life of a child—people in the home, community, school, and church—character education in the school must involve all the adults in the school. This includes counselors, administrators, teachers, media specialists, custodians, cafeteria workers, bus drivers, coaches, and volunteers. The student watches all of us, and our actions and words leave lasting impressions. A great example of this would be Gerald.

Gerald was a bright young man whom I taught several years ago. He was a six-foot, three-inch basketball wizard. He had recently moved to North Carolina from New York and had trouble finding his place in our school. Because he didn't smile much or act overly friendly—he didn't want to appear soft—Gerald intimidated some people. In my U.S. history class, Gerald was a star, with straight As and Bs. He did his work, led class discussions, and always offered great insight into most issues. We had a great relationship. One day, as Gerald entered the classroom, I noticed he looked upset and failed to say hello as he walked by. I knew something was wrong. As class was beginning and students were working on their daily assignment, I walked back to Gerald and asked if everything was okay. His voice cracked as he said "Yeah," and I knew he wasn't telling me the truth, so I invited him into the hallway.

Once outside the door, Gerald started to get upset telling me about what had just happened to him at lunch. He was in the line buying lunch when a friend asked him to get a ketchup for him. Gerald was already at the register and picked up an extra packet of ketchup. He placed the packet next to the register with a quarter, then went on with the ketchup and his lunch. When he was three steps away, the cashier yelled for him to come back. When he did, she accused him of stealing. Gerald told her the situation, believing she had seen him place the money and ketchup down. She called him a liar and a thief, and called the assistant principal over to report him for disobedience, stealing, cutting in line, and insubordination. Gerald had done nothing wrong in the lunch line. As he was telling me this story, he broke down crying. Here was a grown young man sobbing like a baby because of the way he was treated in the cafeteria. Gerald's life was deeply affected by that experience. (Today, Gerald is a successful retail manager and doing well, though he says he will never forget that day.)

All of us know similar stories, most of them good. One of our school secretaries has pictures of perhaps twenty former students hanging beside her desk, each with a special note on the back about how she made a difference in their lives. Looking at those pictures gives her joy every day. All adults in a school are role models, and we are judged not just by what we say and do with students, but also by how we treat each other. There is no unimportant job in a school because we are all looked up to by the students. Don't let anyone forget that fact.

WANT

To be a positive force in the life of our students we have got to want to be there! Our mood, demeanor, and enthusiasm are contagious. I have met thousands of teachers around the country and have yet to meet a single one who reports being in the job for the money. The summer vacations are nice, especially if your own children are of school age, but they're growing shorter and don't nearly make up for all the hours we put in during the school year. If any of us get to the point that we don't want to be there, it's time to get out. Kids know. We can't fool them. As the teacher, we set the mood and the tone for the classroom and our students. If you don't want to be there, then neither do they. This brings to mind a quote from Ralph Waldo Emerson I've often used when coaching: "Nothing great was ever achieved without enthusiasm." The same goes for the classroom and the school as a whole.

Lou Holtz, formerly head football coach at Notre Dame and now at University of South Carolina, once said, "Ability determines what you do. Motivation determines why you do it. Attitude determines how well you do it." We all have the ability. We are licensed professionals. We all have the motivation. It obviously had to do with caring about children to some degree (I'm pretty sure it isn't financial). Our attitude towards our profession, our schools, and our children is what we need to question.

TOGETHER

In the course of a school day, the average student probably comes in contact with at least four to seven teachers, one counselor or librarian, a custodian, and a few other adults, not to mention their parents at home. And chances are those nearly dozen adults never get together to discuss what they can do to help that child to be successful. It's unfortunate, but that's definitely the way of life in most of our high schools today. There just isn't much teamwork among the adults. This is bad for us and our students. It seems the common, unspoken belief among high school teachers (this happens far less at the middle and elementary levels) is that what I do in my classroom is what's important and anything outside my walls is secondary. We each think we are the busiest and hardest working. We think we know what's best, and if we don't, we certainly don't have the time to go talk to all of a kid's teachers. This is a great tragedy because we are making our jobs harder for ourselves and missing an opportunity for greater student success.

I know that even if "Brian" has a great hour in my class, he may go to his next period and have a horrible experience. Then his day has been shot and he has probably forgotten all the positive things from my class. We all know it's even worse when a student has had a bad experience before coming to our class and brings a lot of negative energy for us to deal with.

If Brian is doing great in one or two classes but struggling in his others, all his teachers should get together and share what they know about him. We don't have to wait for a meeting called by guidance or a parent request. As a matter of fact, we're probably better off if we don't let it to get to that point. These meetings don't have to take long or be very formal; they can often be done by questionnaire.

We need to use those coaches, club sponsors, counselors, and favorite teachers to our advantage. In workshops I use a football term to describe this—"gang tackling." That's what I preach to my football players, and it will work with our students as well. As the old saying goes, "None of us are nearly as good as all of us."

CHANGE

John W. Gardner said, "If you have some respect for people as they are, you can be more effective in helping them to become better than they are." That's why we are here—to change lives and help children to become better than they were when they first came to us. At the very least we want them to become more knowledgeable or proficient at a certain subject. Hopefully we can also help them become more knowledgeable about themselves and their responsibilities and to become better people.

As teachers, we change lives and shape perceptions daily. If you have taught even one year and haven't changed a single life, you have wasted your time. I have yet to meet a teacher who hasn't made a lasting change in one or more students' lives...whether they realized it or not.

POSITIVELY

Now the question is, "Are we changing children's lives positively?" Are we being a positive influence? Do our students feel better, or worse, after they leave our classes? Not all that we and our colleagues do is positive. I bet you can think of several instances right now when you've seen children affected negatively in school. I'm not talking about them not passing a test or even a class. I'm talking about instances of children being lied to, disrespected, teased, ridiculed, called stupid, publicly embarrassed...all by a teacher.

We have to do more than just change lives. We have to change them for the better. The great majority of us do that already, and all of us can. Take careful note of this popular piece by Haim Ginott. I first read it in an Ann Landers column, but I've seen it numerous times since. It has helped me shape my mission.

"I've come to the frightening conclusion that I am the decisive element in the classroom. My personal approach creates the climate. My daily mood makes the weather. As a teacher, I possess a tremendous power to make a child's life miserable or joyous. I can be a tool of torture or an instrument of inspiration. I can humiliate or humor, hurt or heal. In all situations, it is my response that decides whether a crisis will be escalated or de-escalated, and a child humanized or dehumanized."

—Haim Ginott

CHAPTER 3

Charlie's Guiding Principles

"If someone listens, or stretches out a hand or whispers a kind word of encouragement, or attempts to understand..., extraordinary things begin to happen."

—Loretta Girzartis

I believe it is important to know what attitudes or principles guide my teaching and thoughts on character education. These are the foundation on which my teaching practices are based. If other teachers want to try something that I do in the classroom, it's important for them to know the basis for my reasoning. These beliefs determine the type of teacher I want to be and am continually working to become.

We Teach CHILDREN

Pretty obvious, huh? I don't think so. Ask a hundred secondary school teachers what they teach. Ninety-nine of them will say something like "history," "physics," or "math." Almost never will you hear a secondary teacher respond that he or she teaches "children." Now ask a group of elementary teachers what they teach and you'll hear them say "first graders," etc. I know it may seem like just a play on words, but it's more than that. Secondary teachers, in both middle and high school, often think of themselves as teachers of a subject, thus putting that curriculum before their children. I've done the same thing myself, and still catch myself saying that I teach U.S. history. In actuality, I teach children—human beings, teenagers— about U.S. history.

It's easy to forget we're teaching children because kids in seventh to twelfth grade start maturing so much physically and socially. When I was coaching middle school football, I had kids bigger than I am, including some with full-grown beards! So many girls come into high school looking like they're 19 or 20 years old, or even older. It's the way they dress, make themselves up, and develop. It is easy for all adults to look at these teenagers, see how grown up they look and try to act, and assume that we can treat them like adults. Well, we can't. The kids may talk a big game and try to convince us they are grown up, but they are not yet there. They are children. They are emotionally and psychologically immature. They are still developing. They need our guidance and help in that development. We mustn't be fooled by the outside package. Kids still need that hug or pat on the back. They are still vulnerable and impressionable. We all know of specific kids who seem hardened, and the words vulnerable and impressionable don't seem to describe them. The adults in these children's lives were either absent or left them to fend for themselves too soon. We can make a big difference by stepping in just the least little bit into their lives. Notice them. Care about them. We don't teach subjects. We teach human beings—CHILDREN!

Teachers Are the KEY—We Can and Do Make a Difference

As a teacher you might have in your classroom anywhere from 20 to 170 children a day, for 180 days. If you aren't making a difference in the lives of many of those children, you are in the wrong profession. But you're not. We do make a difference. We may not always see it immediately, but our influence goes deep and lasts long. I know we're not everything in the lives of our students. They are influenced by their homes, parents—or lack of parents—friends, social groups, the media...the list goes on and on. But, for six or so hours per day the children are entrusted to us. That is often more than their own parents see them. We cannot take our role lightly.

Earlier I wrote about how all the adults in the life of a student play a role in that student's development. Within the school setting, it is the teachers and coaches who have the greatest amount of contact with the children and set the climate for interaction. At school, children take in everything we say and do. They watch us in the hall and in public areas, and they hear us interacting with other students and adults. Principals are vital to the running and atmosphere of the school and are our leaders in the building, but they don't have the daily, constant, one-to-one contact with the children that teachers do. Our support staffs greatly influence the atmosphere of our schools, but they haven't invested in the children the same amount or kind of time that the classroom teacher has invested. Pretty posters and slogans are nice. Motivational speakers can be outstanding. Yet, it is the presence and power of the *teacher* that makes the classroom and ultimately the school.

Real Change Begins with the Climate

In his book, *The Basic School*, Ernest Boyer refers to the school climate as the "Hidden Curriculum." How very true. Many people in education are so keyed into the curriculum that they forget the importance of that classroom and school climate. If the climate of the class is not a positive one, how much learning is going to take place? Not nearly as much as if the classroom climate is civil, inviting, and comfortable. When the climate of our classes is positive, and the children feel secure, respected, confident, and safe, then real learning can take place. If you plant a garden in untilled, unprepared ground, you shouldn't expect much of a crop. Similarly, if you try to teach children in a classroom that has not been tilled with caring, respect, responsibility, and high expectations for all students, you shouldn't expect much learning or maturing.

"Results and responsibility. Not excuses."

—Marva Collins

This Is Not an Add-on, and We Don't Lower Standards

Character education is not an add-on. It is simply what good teachers have been doing for centuries. It is caring about the students and wanting the best for your kids and classroom. Only in this age of cynicism and unbridled paperwork and bureaucracy do we call it an add-on. Because character is more often caught than taught, we all do "character education" every day anyway. Once again, the question arises, how good a job are we doing? Are we modeling good character, respect, and high expectations? If character education is a true add-on for a teacher, then that teacher sadly lacks it and really needs to add it on.

Many people confuse this somehow with lowering the standards for children. Too many view character education, at least initially, as a pleasant, "touchy-feely," warm and fuzzy program. Actually it is just the opposite. We have to hold our children and ourselves to a higher standard. If the old methods of straight lecture and dictating from a text don't work—and they are the least effective ways to teach—we need to change our strategies. They need to reflect more than the common "2x4" teaching style: confined between the two covers of our textbook and inside the four classroom walls. Strategies outside the 2x4 would include service learning, cooperative learning, Paideia coaching, and differentiated instruction. Expectations need to be high for all of our children. They may learn at different rates and in different ways, but we can and must expect great things from them. If we expect less, we will get less.

The challenge comes for many teachers in changing strategies. It's easy for all of us to get into our routine and not change anything, but as each class, year, and generation changes, we have to be willing to change or add some things as well. It's not always easy to step out of and expand our comfort zone, but as Frank Scully so eloquently put it, "Why not go out on a limb? Isn't that where the fruit is?"

> "No one rises to low expectations."
>
> —Carl Boyd

Role Models...Not Necessarily Friends

Role models are individuals that one looks at to emulate. They are people who give us examples of how to live. I agree with Dr. James Comer when he says that parents are a child's first and foremost role models. At the same time, I realize that many people identify celebrities and sports stars as role models—and some of those folks, like Michael Jordan and Wayne Gretzky, are great role models. But we teachers are also role models. Our students watch us constantly. They watch what we do and listen to what we say—even when we don't think they're paying attention. Do your kids notice when you've gotten a haircut or are wearing a new article of clothing? How about when your voice is different, or you have an ink stain or chalk on your back? Of course they do. That's why we as teachers need to take being a role model very seriously. Our children are very impressionable and see us as authority figures, moral leaders, and sometimes as resources for their emotional needs. For those students who don't have strong family lives or otherwise strong support systems, our roles are even larger and more influential. We must not ignore, deny, or minimize that responsibility.

Many teachers, especially new or younger teachers, want to form those important, close relationships with their students by becoming their "friends." Forming positive, close relationships with our students is paramount to classroom success for the teacher, but becoming friends with your students can be costly and detrimental to both the student and the teacher.

I am very close to many of my students. We talk about a lot of things, a great many of which are not related to school at all—relationships, dating, friends, jobs, future, parents, what happened over the weekend, childhood. I wouldn't trade those open, close relationships with my kids for anything. I like to play basketball or football with my students after school or on the weekends when I can. Last summer, the greatest phone message on my answering machine was from one of my kids, Wes, who had just graduated six weeks earlier.

He and some of the fellas were going to go fishing together before they all headed off to college, and they asked if I wanted to go with them. What a great feeling those guys gave me.

As close as I am to so many of my students, they and I realize that I am not one of their "friends." Friends are those people you talk with on the phone all the time, go to parties with, go on vacations with, etc. For too many high school kids, it's who they get in trouble with or ask to buy them beer. That should not be their teacher. There is a definite line. One that is dangerous to cross. I'm a role model my students feel comfortable with and can confide in. I am often a moral compass for my students. It is a great responsibility for all of us. Students don't need more friends. That's too often their problem anyway—too many friends who aren't real friends. They need more role models.

What WE Know About ALL Children

Early in 1998 I was fortunate enough to go through what my school system, Guilford County Schools, calls Comer 102 Training. This training is based upon the School Development Process created by Dr. James P. Comer. This was a great training with a great group of people. Involved were classroom teachers, parents, and administrators from various ethnic and cultural backgrounds, representing rural, suburban, and inner-city schools. One of our small-group exercises (about eight per small group) was to identify and list all of the educational theories we could recall from our college days. I guess we were kind of an "old" group because, after Maslow and Kohlberg, we started to struggle. Alternatively, we decided to list things that we knew about children. We figured that had to be a lot because, among the eight of us, we had more 200 years of experience raising and teaching children. The list we came up with was wonderful because we recognized many important similarities among our children, despite their obvious differences. The top three things on our list were:

1. All children want to be successful.
2. All children want to feel/ be appreciated.
3. All children want to belong.

Isn't that true with your kids? Think about it—doesn't every kid want to be successful? Sure he does. They just go about it in different ways—some kids sell drugs, some study and others cheat, some play sports, some work on cars. Every child wants to be successful and will seek out something—positive or negative—to succeed at. It's one way they get "respect." How about the girl who wears her skirt way too short or her blouse way too low, and has a bad reputation...doesn't she want to feel loved and appreciated? Absolutely. She is just going about it in a way that many of us don't feel is very appropriate and not best for her in the long run. How about kids who join a gang? Don't they want to belong and feel appreciated? Sure. Once again they just chose a different avenue than the football players, cheerleaders, thespians, band members, and "pot heads." All too often recently we have seen the dangerous consequences of children who exhibit extreme behavior because they don't feel they belong.

Sometimes we have to look through the negative actions our kids take and try to determine what it is they are trying to accomplish. Then we can go about showing them a better, safer, and more appropriate way of achieving their ultimate goals—goals just like we all have. One of the greatest speakers I've ever heard, Carl Boyd, once said that the actions of our students are like the tip of an iceberg, and that we as teachers had to be willing to look under the water and see that 90% of the child that exists beneath the surface.

Self-Respect is Greater Than Self-Esteem

Too many people confuse self-respect with self-esteem. They are not the same thing. Self-esteem is feeling good about who you are, but it does not always correlate into something positive. Supposedly drugs make you feel great. Should we give all of our kids drugs and get them high, thinking that then they will succeed in school? Of course not, that is ridiculous. Along the same lines, just passing out happy stickers to every kid every day and telling them they are super won't make them great students. I know a lot of students who would feel good if I never gave notes, homework, tests or quizzes.

Whether or not they learn the material would be a whole different matter.

Self-respect is feeling good and respecting yourself because you have *done* something good. I am very much in support of helping students build their self-respect and giving them opportunities to succeed. Kids are not dumb. They know when we are rewarding them for nothing. Greater satisfaction and sense of accomplishment come when children work for their success. It isn't really success if they did not earn it, and they know that. As a teacher, I feel it is my responsibility to help build my students up. They must do the work. I just provide them with the tools and opportunity to be successful. Otherwise, it's just like me looking in the mirror and telling myself, "Charlie, you are slim and trim." It isn't going to happen if I don't do some work.

I don't want to put down every program out there today that espouses self-esteem as a tool for student success. I think if you take a look at most of those programs, what they are really talking about is self-respect, or as I once heard Eric Schapps call it, "earned esteem." Don't automatically discount programs that talk about or feature self-esteem; just check to see what they're really talking about. I think most of the teaching techniques and practices I describe later in the book have as a goal to help develop the self-respect of my students.

Two Main Reasons for Dropping Out

Bobbie Cobb is one of the greatest teachers, counselors, and educators in the world. For the last eleven years she has been a drop-out prevention counselor at my school. When I first went to Southwest she was one of those people I could tell right away was in tune with the children and genuinely cared about them. I wanted to be like Bobbie Cobb.

She has taught me a great deal about teaching and children, always sharing ideas, programs, and tips with me. One piece of information she shared with me several years ago has always stuck in my mind, and still relates to so many things we do with and talk about concerning children. Bobbie shared with me the two main reasons for kids dropping out of school. They are 1) no connection/no support, and 2) low academic performance.

So simple, and oh so powerful! Those two things are why we want to teach students. If we can find a way to connect with our students, show them that we do care and support, and then find ways to raise and strengthen their academic performance—what a difference we could make! Can you imagine what would happen if every teacher and educator in a school, as well as every student, committed to fight against those two things? We might not ever lose another child. With the right tools, we can build hope.

Discipline

Discipline and maintaining civility in a classroom are essential for any effective practice or learning to take place. I know you can form close relationships with your students and still maintain a strong level of order and civility in your classroom. It is an absolute essential—nothing I do or want to try will ever work if I don't have discipline in my room. That doesn't mean I try to evoke fear in my students, but I demand respect for ourselves and each other, and I encourage a sense of urgency about learning.

Discipline is the biggest problem most teachers face. Early in my career I had the same problems all new teachers encounter, but I became a stronger disciplinarian over the years through practice and because it was such an important element in the work of master teachers and principals I admired. From them I learned that I didn't have to be popular. Having a consistent disciplinarian—firm but fair—is what children really want. Once I began practicing that, I started to become a better teacher.

Here are a few thoughts that guide my actions regarding discipline:

1. Discipline is something I do for my kids, not to them. Children want and like structure. If they are not used to it at home or if they go all day without it in other classes, they may resist it at first. But once they see that my classroom rules and procedures are established for the success and enjoyment of the class, they come along quickly.

2. I enjoy the idea of "killing them with kindness." I try not to lose my temper and fly off the handle. If I lose my control, it's not going to help them regain theirs. (If I can limit myself to no more that four episodes a year of flying off the handle, it has been a good year. We all have our moments!) We have to realize that we really can't control our kids. All we can control is ourselves. We must hope that our actions will create a positive climate and prevent confrontations from escalating. I discipline with a smile and suggest ways my kids can do things differently. Saying "please" and "thank you" helps a lot.

3. I remind my kids not to mistake kindness for weakness. I am firm, but fair. All students appreciate that. I don't just dictate—if something seems unfair to them, I take time to explain the issue.

4. My classroom discipline has been helped tremendously by the "Three Rs Test," which I learned from Dr. Jim Fitzpatrick of Vermont. When I must discipline students, I ask myself if the consequences I give are Reasonable, Related, and Respectful. When my disciplinary actions pass this test, it becomes a win-win situation for both me and my students.

The Golden Rule

I try to teach my kids as I wish I'd been taught. For example, I almost never give them homework on the weekends. Why? Because I don't like doing schoolwork on the weekends. My students also have families, work obligations, and private lives. My kids gladly work hard through the week because of my weekend policy. I avoid giving tests on Mondays because I hated them as a student. I also make sure my blackboard is clean and my handwriting is legible. These things may not sound like a big deal, but my students have told me that they appreciate them greatly. Little things can make a surprisingly big difference.

CHAPTER 4

Techniques and Practices for the Classroom

Handshake!

"Thank you"

Coach's Corner

The Away Game

Physical Environment

Daily Assignment

Celebrate a Classmate

Grading Their Own Tests
and Quizzes

Partner Tests

Random Acts of Kindness

Test & Quiz Retakes

A-B-C-Incomplete

T.E.A.M.

Procedures and Their Practice

Seating Charts

Day One Letter

Quote of the Week

ABO Bucks

My House Activity

Bits of Teaching Wisdom
I've Seen Work

The classroom techniques and activities I describe in the following pages are explained in the way I use them. You may have to adjust some of them to your particular classroom, students, personality, and teaching style. I learned many of them from other people and have tweaked them a bit to fit my situation. You well know that each classroom or group of students is different. Not all these techniques will work as well for you, or they may work great in first period composition but bomb in fourth period composition. Others will work better for you than they have for me. Keep in mind that becoming a very effective teacher is a process—it takes time and steady work, making mistakes and making improvements. I don't think it comes "naturally" to anyone, or that some have it and some don't. I make a daily effort to make my classroom a true learning center where students want to be. I've gotten a lot better than I was ten years ago, and still have a bunch to learn!

Though I am a high school teacher, I believe most of these techniques and practices would work well in the elementary and middle school levels as well. I have done numerous presentations at all three levels, and often get calls or letters afterward reporting the success of the techniques at the younger levels.

If you see some ideas you'd like to try, you don't have to wait until next year, next semester, or next week. Go ahead and give something new a try tomorrow, or as soon as you prepare for it. Give it a good, honest effort—and keep at it until it becomes ingrained in class procedure. When you start something new and different, especially something that shows your heart, the students will need some time to determine if you really mean what you're doing. They'll come on board in time.

Many of these activities and techniques you can try in your classroom tomorrow! There's no time like the present to start improving your classroom, your students' lives, or your school!

Handshake!

*Models respect, integrity, trust,
cooperation, connection*

This may be the slightest and easiest change you make to your day and routine, but it may also be the greatest. There is no trick. All I'm talking about is simply shaking the hand of all your students as they enter the classroom! In the half of a second you took to shake that hand, you had a direct, meaningful, personal, and individual connection with that student. It is a chance to connect with every single student every day! Hal Urban calls it transferring positive energy at the door. Harry Wong says it's the only way to start every class. A simple handshake makes a personal connection between you and each student, fosters a respect and integrity, and begins a relationship.

Think about what a handshake is—a greeting, a symbol recognized worldwide for partnership and togetherness. Look at it throughout history. The handshake has ended wars, obtained great wealth, created powerful alliances. The refusal of a handshake has led to devastation, death, and demise! Handshakes are unique and often personalized. It says what kind of person you are. I remember my dad telling me since I was a small child about the importance of a firm handshake and what it said about your character.

What if you or your students aren't comfortable with a handshake? Then you might want to substitute it with a high-five, or even a touch on the shoulder. If you have any students who clearly don't want to be touched, then don't touch them. Respect their space and comfort level. They will usually become more receptive over time.

If you don't get 'em at the door, walk up and down the aisles when you enter the room to shake the hands of the kids you missed. They will deeply appreciate the time and connection. Shaking the hands of your students daily may take up a whole minute of your class, but the benefits could last forever!

You can even make it into a lesson if you want. My economics class and I spent half of a period one day talking about the value of a good handshake in the business world, on job interviews, meeting a date's father—all the ways it can be a positive, valuable human resource. We practiced it regularly the rest of the year. Taking those few seconds for a bit of personal touch with each student—and doing it like you enjoy doing it—will make a big difference in your classroom throughout your school year.

TIP: One way to build upon this would be to practice various styles of handshakes—business, casual, formal, etc. Take a couple of minutes to talk with your kids about the various styles and why/how they might be used, and what they mean to the other person. Throw in the occasional high five for extra excitement and positive energy on test days.

> "Every moment is a golden one for him who has the vision to recognize it as such."
>
> —Henry Miller

Saying "Thank you"
Models respect, appreciation, caring, responsibility

Is there any more important, positive two-word phrase in the world? We probably all teach our own children at home to say "thank you" to everyone any time we receive something, just as you were probably reminded hundreds of times as a child: "What do you say?" Most of us probably try to model at home for our children, but how often do we model it at school by saying "thank you" to our students? Once again, something so simple can make all the difference in the world in your classroom climate and in relationships with your students!

I discovered the value of "thank you" in the classroom several years ago with "Stefanie," a bright young woman in my U.S. history class. An underachiever whose single mom was an airline flight attendant, Stefanie was home alone quite a bit—a tough situation for any teenager! Though she was basically a good girl, she had questionable friends, by parent and counselor standards, and would definitely be considered "at-risk." She was tough, a loner, and quite sarcastic to protect her fragile ego. I loved her!

On an interim report midway through the second quarter, I put Stefanie down for a B+, and in the comment section wrote "Thank you" with a smiley face next to it. I was in a hurry and didn't have time to write more. I was not thinking of it as a "teaching strategy." At the end of class, after I returned the interims, Stefanie came up to me as I was sitting at my desk straightening up. She held out her report and, in a strong tone, asked "What's this?"

"What's what?" I replied, not knowing what she was referring to. She pointed to her report and said, "The thank you." I told her I had written it because I knew she was working hard, completing all of her assignments in five other classes, working a job after school, taking care of her household all by herself, and still doing well in my class. I told her I appreciated what she was going through and accomplishing—that's what I meant by the "thank you." Her confused expression broke into a beautiful smile, and a sense of pride, mixed with relief, came across her face. She said that hardly anyone ever thanked her for anything, and certainly never a teacher. I thought she was going to cry. Heck, I thought I might cry. Ever since that day, Stefanie and I have had a close relationship and certain bond. "Thank you" made all the difference in the world to her!

I had never thought of thanks as an educational tool, but since I saw the difference it made to Stefanie, I use it every chance I get. Since that time, hundreds of students have made comments to me similar to Stefanie's. They *love* feeling appreciated. Students appreciate when we realize all the things they do and how they too must juggle their time and efforts. The feeling that I notice and appreciate their situation changes their whole outlook about the class, and about me as a teacher.

Saying "thank you" to our students builds a mutual respect, a sense of caring and empathy, and that appreciation is one more great thing to build a relationship upon.

TIP: It never hurts to tell your kids "I don't know" or "I'm sorry, I was wrong" either. Remember our students hold stereotypes about teachers. They often think of us as aloof know-it-alls. To admit that we don't know something or that we too make mistakes will help develop a comfortable atmosphere in the class. I'm never afraid to tell my kids, "I don't know, but I can help us find out." As long as you are sincere, your students will return the feeling.

"The little things? The little moments? They aren't little."

—Jon Kabat-Zinn

Coach's Corner
Models respect, trustworthiness, caring

My coach's corner has always been something I thought was important for me to do as a teacher. It's simply a corner of my room, often the corner where I have my desk, where I put up things on the wall or shelves that are a reflection of me as an individual—pictures of my family, team pictures, my children's artwork, Michael Jordan pictures, Redskin stuff, awards and certificates...you get the idea. This is a part of my room where my kids can learn more about me. They can see me as a real person who likes to play, laugh, and have fun just like they do. I'm not just some impersonal adult in the front of the room telling them what to do. They get to see me as a father, husband, friend, fan, and professional. My kids have always loved to ask me about the things in the coach's corner. It has led to some great discussions about more than the textbook, as well as some good basketball games with my kids after school!

Please keep in mind the stereotype that students have about all teachers before they even walk in our rooms. They have this image that we're non-social beings who live and breathe our subject matter, grading papers twenty-four hours a day. They come in with a preconceived negative impression of us, before we even open our mouths. Sadly, some teachers actually live down to that negative expectation, feeling that they have to be hard on the kids the first few weeks to gain control. I don't agree with that philosophy. I think the student-teacher relationship built on mutual respect, trust, and caring will go much further than one based on fear and intimidation. First impressions go a long way—especially with kids.

I remember the first time I realized that teachers were normal— semi-normal, anyway, able to laugh and joke—was during my student teaching my senior year of college! I was amazed and relieved too. I decided then I would do something in my own classroom to let my students know who I really was. My coach's corner was it. It's good for me, too. I enjoy looking at it, seeing many of the things that are important in my life. School takes up a lot of time—time I could be at home with my family. Having the coach's corner lets me have a little of my family with me all day long.

TIP: Harry Wong suggests putting up your diploma, awards, certificates, etc. in your room. This might be a great thing to add to your corner. You want people to know you for who you are away from the classroom as well, and it's worthwhile to let them know you are a true professional. I've done this with various teaching and coaching awards. My students always comment on those things, too. It will give a great total picture of who you are when people can see you both personally and professionally.

> "The most wasted of all days is that during which one has not laughed."
>
> —Nicolas Chamfort

The Away Game

Models respect, trustworthiness, caring, empathy

The "away game" is me going to see my students on their turf. The classroom is a teacher's turf, where we are comfortable and in charge. The away game refers to going to see our students where they work, play a sport, or participate in any extra-curricular activity. Then we're in a situation where the student feels more comfortable, a little more in charge. When we take the time to go to a band performance or a play our students are in, we make a powerful impression. They realize we are taking our time to go see them, and they're terrifically impressed. Make sure they know you're there. Tell them they did a great job. Now they know you care about them as more than just a test score. You have immediately improved that relationship, both in class and out. Possible behavior problems will often cease, simply because that student knows that you care about him or her in particular.

Many of my high school students work. They love it when I stop by their place of employment. Then we have switched roles. Now I'm the one who doesn't know everything about the situation, and they get to "teach" me. I'll never forget going to eat at Shoney's one night with my family. A BEH student I'll call "Gus" was our waiter. I didn't even realize he waited tables there, but he made us his star guests. He worked hard to make sure we knew that he had mastered his job. Gus introduced his manager to us, talked about school and things he needed to do better. Here was a kid who was BEH and in perpetual trouble at school now being the perfect employee. He was working hard, earning a decent wage, and knew what he was talking about. That encounter improved our relationship for the better. I had positive, personal things I could ask him about, and he could always ask about my family and when I was coming back to Shoney's. The power of the away game should never be underestimated.

TIP: It is very helpful to have your kids fill out information sheets or cards early in the year. Have them give information such as family members, hobbies, jobs, goals, etc., not just school stuff. Take some time to get to know them on paper; then surprise them by taking an interest in their out-of-class life.

"Men are all alike in their promises. It is only in their deeds that they differ."

—Moliere

Physical Environment
Promotes determination and motivation

The physical environment of a classroom is tremendously important in determining the climate, atmosphere, and mood of the class. When I say environment, I'm referring to your walls, bulletin boards, chalk boards, desks, and sounds. This is an area where most elementary teachers do an outstanding job. Their decorations are bright and fun. There are numerous things on each wall. There is lots of color. Research shows that children's creativity and active thinking are increased when they are visually stimulated. Secondary teachers, high school more so than middle, need to do a better job imitating their elementary-level peers. I've heard many high school teachers say, "That stuff is childish" or "This isn't elementary school."

They are right. The posters and bulletin boards in middle and high schools need to be geared towards the older students.

A former principal of mine, Earl Crotts, used to say he loved coming into my classroom because as soon as he walked in, he could tell what subjects I taught. There are historical front pages all over, a large U.S. flag, numerous pictures of historical figures, along with many motivational banners and character posters. My personal theory always has been that I may not be exciting every day and every topic may not light them on fire, but, by golly, they can always learn something by reading my walls.

My students love looking around and reading the headlines and quotes. They like the color, too. I remember in college being told not to put much up on the walls because it would be distracting to kids, especially those with learning differences and/or attention deficit disorder. I also remember how boring my room looked that first year with only a couple things on each wall. Now it's often those exceptional students who are most turned on to the class by the walls and decor. It helps them focus, and if their attention does shift visually, it shifts to something educational, making it easier for me to get them back on task. I also keep in mind the importance of first impressions, and each day when kids walk into our classrooms they see the room first!

CLASS NOTES—Along those same lines, I have found that the way we present information for them to take notes on has a tremendous impact on students. Taking notes was never my favorite thing, nor is it my students', so I try to liven that up a bit. I give a lot of notes, usually using the overhead screen. I always write in blue or black, but make a point to underline major points in red, and star important dates, people, etc. in green or purple. I usually write my headings in strong balloon letters, with color. All through grade school and college, I couldn't stand it when teachers gave notes that I couldn't read because of their bad handwriting—so I make it a point to print neatly and large enough to read easily. My students greatly appreciate it.

When I'm showing notes to support my lectures, I almost always uncover only a couple of lines at a time and try to give them time to complete copying and reading what they just wrote before I resume talking. Sometimes kids will ask you just to let them copy the whole page so they can get it over with, but that's counter-productive because when they get done copying they often shut down, not listening as well to your explanation and points of emphasis. Hundreds of students have told me they love the way I give notes because they can remember the material better when we do notes in short clips, explaining and discussing each little piece.

For the last four years I have been hanging my overhead screen across a corner in the front of the room, next to the chalkboard. This location has been a great use of space and has allowed me to fully use all of my chalkboard without having to cover anything up. It allows me more room to give notes, use maps, pictures or whatever. It's also something different than the standard front-and-center location. Kids do like a change of pace.

The chalkboard is also a great tool that many of us don't fully utilize. Besides the things I write on the board, such as daily assignments and things due this week—which I'll explain later—the appearance of the board is surprisingly important to students. Is it clean or is it dusty and chalky from days or weeks of erasing? My board is washed every single day, so that the writing is strong, bright, and easy to read. As with my overhead notes, I try to use balloon or decorative block lettering for note headlines, and I use a lot of color. Students say they love my board and notes, that I make it easy for them to read and pay attention to what is written. I love to use bright-colored art chalk. Strong red, purple, green, blue, neon yellow, and black are great on the board. The clean board and colored chalk do take more time on my part, but the payoff in appearance, atmosphere, and student work level is well worth it.

MUSIC—I have found music to be an essential component of my classroom climate. I use it in two ways. First, I always have music playing as students enter the classroom. Usually, I play a classical symphonic or piano tape. This creates a relaxing atmosphere. The great majority of my kids always ask early in the year if I will play this or that radio station or their tapes if they bring them in, but I don't do it. You will rarely get twenty or thirty kids all to agree on one type of music. Plus, I'm trying to set a tone. Exposing them to classical music isn't bad either! Within weeks they love the music and always ask me to play it if they are doing vocabulary or writing assignments. Music really does seem to soothe the savage breast—the kids always work quietly and productively.

A key benefit of playing music as the kids come into class is that it sets my class apart. Before I ever say a word, my kids know that there is something special and different about this class! They like it!

I also mix up the music, too. Often on Fridays, I'll play a mix of rock, pop, soul, oldies, rap, top forty. I made a tape of motivational songs, upbeat current songs with a message, that my kids love to hear on Fridays. To give you an idea, that tape includes Aretha Franklin's "Respect," James Brown's "I Feel Good," TLC's "Waterfalls," and Coolio's "The Winner." Music is great for setting the mood/tone of the class, and it can be a great pick-me-up during a long spell of dreary days.

TIP: It's important not only that our rooms look good and inviting, but also that we do. I'm a strong believer in teachers dressing like professionals. I don't mean wearing suits or jackets and ties every day, but rather wearing nice, clean, pressed clothes every day—never shorts, blue jeans, or ultra-casual shirts. We aren't kids. We are role models and should dress appropriately for the authority figures we are. I always dress comfortably, and only wear a tie once or twice a week, but I do dress like I'm going to work. Your students will respect this and notice your personal appearance as quickly as anything.

> "Success is doing what you can, with what you have, where you are."
>
> —Theodore Roosevelt

Daily Assignment
Develops responsibility

This technique is one I heard about from reading and listening to tapes by Harry Wong. It has been a tremendous technique for me, and one that everyone should use. The daily assignment is the action of giving your students a short assignment to work on at the beginning of class each day. It should be posted in the same place every day. My daily assignments are designed to take only five to ten minutes, and to introduce my students to that day's lesson. I have used this technique daily for the last six years and will for the next thirty!

Having a daily assignment for my kids encourages—actually demands—responsibility. My kids know that every day when they come in they are to read their daily assignment first thing and get started. Never is there a question of "What are we supposed to do?" or "What are we going to talk about today?" They know. There is no guessing or delay by confusion. They like this because there are no surprises, and they gain confidence because they can prepare themselves. I benefit because I get five to ten minutes to take care of those tasks we all have to do at the start of each period—taking roll, writing admit slips, signing notes. It also gives me time to walk around the class and give some individual time when needed.

My students do not come to me naturally programmed to carry out this daily responsibility. We have to practice it at the beginning of the school year (and usually after winter and spring breaks as well).

The strongest testament I can give to the value of the daily assignment and the responsibility that it helps foster comes from my first period class last year. On this particular day I happened to have an 8 a.m. meeting on the other side of town. I'd made arrangements for a co-worker to cover my class that morning. I ended up getting to school about 9:15. Classes began at 8:30. When I walked into class, my students were working diligently and quietly. I looked around to thank my co-worker for covering for me, but did not see him. I asked my kids where he had gone, and they said neither he nor any other teacher had been to class yet! I was happily amazed. I asked them how they knew what to do and why they were so quiet. Their reply was simply that they always knew where the assignment was and what to do. They figured I or someone would be in sometime. I was so pleased and proud I told them they had earned an extra 100 points on their next pop quiz. They had shown responsibility, respect, self-discipline, and integrity—all on their own. Our routine procedures and the daily assignment had helped make these high school juniors pro-active, independent, and responsible learners.

TIP: A useful addition to the daily assignment would be what former teacher, administrator, and professor Dr. Max Thompson calls the "Essential Question." This is a focus question written on the board to show students where they are headed for the day and what they're responsible for learning by the end of class. Dr. Thompson's E.Q. is often aligned with the major curriculum objective for the day. The Daily Assignment tells your students what they're responsible for as soon as they enter class, and using the E.Q. places responsibility on your students for their learning that day. This can make the daily assignment a great one-two punch.

"Children develop character by what they see, by what they hear, and by what they are repeatedly led to do."
—James Stenson

Celebrate a Classmate
Develops respect, caring, motivation

This activity may just be the best thing I did with my classes all last year. This idea I heard about from Dr. Phil Vincent, who told me about this super activity done by a California teacher, Hal Urban. When I first heard this affirmation activity described, I thought it sounded kind of "fluffy" and had my doubts, but I'm always willing to try new activities that might help my classroom. Well, Celebrate a Classmate went so well that as soon as I did it with my first class, I ran to tell the teacher in the room next to me about this wonderful activity she had to do with her class! This really was one of the best, if not THE best thing I did all last year.

Here's how I set it up as a daily assignment. I wrote on the board that I wanted them to Celebrate a Classmate. They were to write something nice or something they appreciated or admired about someone in class. At first, the kids had questions. I told them to write something nice about somebody, but not necessarily their best friend in class. I gave a few simple examples to get their minds into this mode because few high school kids ever do this type of thing. They had to put their names on their papers, but I promised I would not identify any authors when I read the papers. I didn't want to embarrass anyone. My students thought deeply and wrote quietly.

As I started to look these over myself, I was really pleased, but when I read them aloud the effects enlightened my life! The comments written down included, "Derik has a nice smile," "Ian is smart and funny," "Steven makes me laugh every day," "Courtney is always nice to everyone," and "Crystal is here today. I have missed her." You should have seen their bright eyes and smiles when they heard their name and what others thought of them! It made everyone feel great—appreciated and special. Crystal's reaction was the best. She'd been out of school sick for three or four days, and this happened to be her first day back. When I read, "Crystal is here today. I have missed her," her eyes lit up like beacons and the most beautiful smile I have ever seen in a classroom came across her face. She and I both melted. The young man sitting behind Crystal, Tim, had written this celebration. They were classmates, but had never been close friends. When Tim saw Crystal's smile and eyes as she looked around the class to see who might have written this, a warm smile came across his face. As my kids were leaving class at the end of the period, I stopped Crystal and asked her why she seemed so surprised and delighted. She said she hadn't thought anyone, apart from me, even noticed when she was gone! Now she knew differently. My students learned many things that day, but one big thing was that they do matter to other folks and do make an impression on others.

Many people ask what happens to the kids who don't get written about—aren't their feelings hurt? That's possible, but the way I used this last year, I was able to avoid that. I did this about once every three or four weeks, and I told my kids to write about someone different each time. They were very sensitive to others in the class, and many went out of their way to write nice things about classmates who might not have been included yet. As another safeguard against hurt feelings, at the end of the semester I wrote a celebration about each individual in class and read these aloud.

Celebrate a Classmate is something I will do for the rest of my career. The way it builds a sense of caring and family in the classroom is phenomenal. It brings a lot to the class atmosphere.

TIP: Along the same line as this activity, and used in the same manner, is to have your kids describe or write down something good that has happened to them in the last two weeks (or any length of time). I love doing this because it forces kids to look for the positive. We all know how readily teenagers want to focus on negative things. One of my students, Brad, told me that nothing good has happened to him. I prodded him a little, and he eventually came up with, "I'm living." As I read these aloud

in class I was quick to respond, "That beats the alternative." He agreed.

Grading THEIR OWN Tests and Quizzes
Develops honesty, trust, responsibility, respect, achievement

When I first heard about this technique, I immediately had the same thought, concern, or doubt that you probably just had: "Won't they cheat?" I've since found out that no, they won't. In the five or six years I've been using this, I found one student cheating and suspected only two others. That's out of probably 900+ students in that time period. I believe if a child is going to cheat, he or she is going to cheat anyway. I also strongly believe in these words of Booker T. Washington, "Few things help an individual more than to place responsibility upon him and to let him know that you trust him."

The sound academic merit to this practice is well documented. Every study ever done on academic feedback states that the sooner a student receives the feedback, the more useful it becomes. You can't get any feedback sooner than immediate feedback. That's what students get when they grade their own tests and quizzes. They get to grade their own work immediately, or the next day at the latest! Students immediately get to see what mistakes they may have made and see what the correct answers are and why.

When I do this, I go over the questions and answers patiently, and I allow all the time they need to answer any questions. I take time to explain questions that may have led to any problem. The students love learning from their mistakes and having those explained while the material is fresh in their minds. This part of the learning process helps greatly come time for the next test or quiz. The additional learning also carries over to the end-of-course test. Achievement is directly and positively affected. I also let, and often demand, my students retake work that is subpar. This practice helps here as well. What we have now is immediate feedback, increased and active learning, and what is even more important, "mastery learning." Achievement is up. Self-respect is up. Responsibility is increased.

There is also a benefit to the teacher. I have not always gotten papers back to students in a very timely fashion. I still don't always, but this practice has helped greatly. As a father, husband, and coach, I also have other responsibilities just as important as my students' papers. It has not always been possible for me to get papers back the next day or two. I'm happy if I get them back in the same week in many cases. How many of us have done this?—pack up and take papers home to grade, get home and not have or make the time to grade them (often because we're too tired, too busy, or else there is a good game or show on television), take them back to school thinking you might get to grade them the next day, you don't...so you start the whole cycle over again—sometimes for days! I call it the "Grading Papers Two-Step." I used to be the master. Now with letting my kids grade some of their own tests and quizzes, I do a whole lot less two-steppin'. The kids are learning more and I'm doing less! You can't beat it! I consider it simply working smarter, not harder.

Let me clarify how I use this. I don't do this every time. I do it when I can, depending upon the style of test or quiz. Obviously you can't do this with essays or many short-answers tests. I don't do this until after we've been in school for several weeks and I've established a positive atmosphere and relationship with the class. Then we have a degree of trust and respect to build upon. The first time or two I did this, my kids were in shock. They wanted to change writing utensils or papers, just to show me they weren't cheating. I told them I trusted them and explained how it would be better for their learning. They couldn't believe that a teacher was trusting them to grade their own papers. This is where the Booker T. Washington quotation comes in. Students love knowing that you trust them. My kids work to make sure they don't abuse that trust.

TIP: I knew an English teacher once who would simply write on essays and other written assignments the number of errors that she found on each page or per paragraph. She then returned the work to her kids and had them find and correct their own mistakes. Then she would grade the work based on their improved efforts. She had the students do the work and learn on their own, holding them to a higher standard. I've done this frequently and have had great results too.

"Few things help an individual more than to place responsibility upon him and to let him know that you trust him."
—Booker T. Washington

Partner Tests
Develops respect, responsibility, achievement

When I first used this technique about five years ago, it was one of the best examples I had ever seen of active, participatory learning. It still is. The partner test is also a great way for the high school teacher to incorporate cooperative learning. I learned it from a Clare Lemeres workshop and have used it and loved it ever since.

A partner test is a normal test, but the student has a partner to discuss answers with. I have always given the partners one test and one answer sheet. Both students use the same answer sheet and get the same grade. I've had a handful of students who prefer not to have a partner, so I let them work alone. I don't force anyone to do a partner test. I've also had the situation where uneven numbers forced me to allow a group of three students to work together. They all get the same grade.

I set up my first partner test of the year as I would any other. We have a test review or study guide the day before the test. On test day everything runs as usual right up until I give the test out. Once my students are ready, I surprise them by telling them to get with a partner. Are they ever startled! (Of course a majority of people head directly to the straight-A students. Laugh it off and reiterate that each student is to have only one partner!) Once everyone has a partner, I have them spread out around the room, so the pairs may talk quietly without disturbing other groups. I tell them how the test works: one answer sheet, one grade, and they must whisper. I say they are to discuss each answer with their partners and work together to come up with the best answer.

Before I tried this for the first time, I had my doubts about how well it might work and what level of chaos would ensue. I am happy to report that the first time I used this, I was hooked for life. In every partner test I gave them, they cooperated, discussed historical theory, and really analyzed the questions and issues before them. To my mind, this was the best example of active learning and application I had ever seen. My students were actually discussing class lectures and notes. It made me feel good to realize that they had really been paying close attention. The partner test worked and has continued to work like a dream.

I do not make every test a partner test. I use it maybe once every four to six weeks. After that first time, when I let my kids pick their partners, I have chosen for them. I do it randomly, not necessarily trying to pair the best test taker with the worst. I don't try to set anyone up to pass or fail. Not knowing who their partner will be the next time puts a little bit of peer pressure on students. No one wants to look like a dummy. Kids love the opportunity to work together—cooperative learning is very natural—and they strive to do their best.

TIP: I was recently speaking in South Carolina and a high school science teacher there told me she did partner tests but added a twist. The pairs of students have two answer sheets instead of one. This way, if there is a dispute over a question and the partners can't decide which is correct, they each have the freedom to go on their own with that one. This was a great adaptation I've since used.

"Teamwork works."

Random Acts of Kindness
Develops caring, integrity, respect

I think we've all heard of this activity/assignment, but not enough of us use it. What this entails is simply assigning your students to commit a "random act of kindness." This may be doing something to help out at home, helping a neighbor or friend, opening a door for a teacher or stranger...anything, just to be spontaneously generous and helpful. Unfortunately we're now conditioned to hearing about random acts of violence. It will strengthen our communities to challenge our students and ourselves to commit random acts of kindness. Great lessons will be learned by your students.

I do this by assigning a random act of kindness (RAK) as a homework assignment for a week. On Friday of that week they turn in to me in writing what RAK they performed and for whom. I count this act as a homework grade. We often take time to discuss how other people feel when we perform these acts for them, and how helping others makes us feel. I've met teachers who expand on this by having their kids keep a RAK Log of three to five acts of kindness per week.

There are a lot of ways you can use this assignment, and you'll enjoy a raft of unexpected benefits. You'll have fun, your kids will have fun, but wait till you hear the comments from parents and other teachers in the school! They love it, too. Whenever I make this assignment a priority, we really help our overall school climate. I need to do this a lot more!

With the numerous school shootings in recent years, I've used RAK in my classroom to examine how our students and teachers might be able to help prevent some of these tragedies. In discussing these frightening acts of violence, I introduced RAK to my kids and we discussed and came up with ways we might be able to prevent an act of violence at our school. The discussions turned into role-playing scenarios! I would have a student come to the front of class and sit up against the wall, hands to his face, knees up, looking withdrawn and depressed. I asked my kids if they'd ever seen any-one in our school who they thought looked like this for a while. They all raised their hands—yes. Then I suggested that this person might be so lonely and depressed that he too might act out in a vio-lent way. I asked what they could do to help before anything like that ever happened.

Many said, "Nothing—just mind your own business." Others came up with simple things such as just saying hello and smiling, or starting small talk. We practiced some of that, and then I asked what could be the worst response to their friendly overture. They decided the worst that could happen would be to get cussed at and told to mind their own business. (We didn't think being shot or stabbed was a very likely reaction when you act friendly toward someone.) We agreed that if that negative scenario took place, it probably wouldn't be the first time they'd heard a cuss word and that they could just walk off. What was more important, we decid-ed that the best-case scenario would be making a difference in some-body's life and perhaps prompting that person to get some help. Now just because a kid is lonely and depressed doesn't mean he will shoot up a school, but no act of kindness is wasted. Kind words and deeds can save lives. That was a great day of learning for my kids.

TIP: I know there are many ways to have students do random acts of kindness. I've heard of two variations I'm eager to try. A friend has her kids do the same thing, but they must record their acts in a journal and write about them. What a great way to have students process their actions. A middle school teacher told me she had her kids perform random acts of kindness in teams to build upon both cooperative learning and service learning.

> They who give have all things; they who withhold have nothing.
>
> —Hindu Proverb

Test and Quiz Retakes
Develops integrity, achievement, perseverance, responsibility

This is one of my favorite practices. I have used it for years and tailored it to suit my needs and style. In my class, students can retake any test or quiz they want, until they get the grade they want. I don't average the grades of the two or three or four...I give them the full grade of the one they do best on. I give them the same test or quiz each time, and I don't alter the material unless I feel the system is being abused or taken advantage of. There is some extra work for me, and I record grades in my gradebook in pencil—until my kids have the grade they want.

The first time I create a test or quiz, it's a good one. It covers all of the objectives and materials I have taught. I put a good bit of effort into creating tests and quizzes. I'm not going to go crazy making up new ones for retakes. I want to test my kids on the material I have shared with them. My goal is their mastery of the subject material. I don't shoot for a grading curve or anything like that. If all my kids get As, fantastic. I don't care how it looks. I care if they learn or not. This practice helps instill that mastery learning.

Now there are catches: 1) Students must come in to make up work on their own time—before school, after school, or during their lunch, and 2) I may rearrange questions if needed.

This policy is stated to students and given to parents from day one. By making parents aware of this policy at the outset, I get tremendous parent support. Parents know that their children can succeed if they want to put forth the effort. It places the responsibility on the child.

If you put this technique together with having students grade their own tests and quizzes, your students can't help but succeed. That doesn't mean that they will all use the system to their advantage, but at least they know that their grade and success in the class is primarily up to them.

TIP: A great way to organize this and to develop responsibility is at the beginning of the year (or when you begin this practice) to designate a specific day or two when your kids can come in for their retakes. Make this non-negotiable. It takes away the guessing and excuse game for kids as to when they can come in to do a retake. They now know the time and day. This will make it easier and more structured for the students and helpful to you as well.

"Mediocrity does not inspire men to greatness."

—Zarienga

A-B-C...Incomplete
Develops integrity, determination, achievement

This technique or system is a challenge to our standard mode of thinking. In this case, you simply stop accepting work that is below average. Establish the grading system for your class that ends at the lowest possible C. I started doing this because I know that none of my students are below average when they try. I decided to stop letting them get by with near-failing marks. They are better than that. I'm also keenly aware of the effect that high expectations have on our children. This is a great way to reflect those high expectations.

Before I started using this system, I went to my principal and got his approval. He was curious to see if it would work and how it would be accepted. Next, I wrote a letter to my students and their parents, explaining my new grade policy. I approached both my students and their parents with my belief that all children can learn and succeed. My new policy would require that anyone who makes below a C on ANY work—homework, writing assignments, vocabulary lists, anything—must redo it. Any student who fails to make up his or her work is given a grade of incomplete until better work is completed. If it comes to the end of the grading period and there are more than two things not yet done, the grade on the report card will be an I—Incomplete. If the work is then not done within two weeks, all incomplete assignments are counted as 0, and a grade will be averaged and given. So when all is said and done, a student may actually receive a D or F, but it's the very last resort—parents and students have been made aware of the situation more than once.

My success with this has been terrific. Parents love it. Students like knowing that they can pass a subject, even if they have never had success in it before. I love it because the responsibility for success lies in the hands of the students. I wish I could tell you that all my students have made a C or higher since I started using this technique several years ago, but I can't. Some kids have made the choice to fail or perform at substandard levels. We talk frequently about the lifelong implications for making those choices, but some haven't caught on.

The only drawback to the A-B-C-Incomplete system is that it can mean a little more work for me, but the success of the students is worth it. This technique has helped motivate many students and gotten parents more involved, and improved my classroom atmosphere and relationships. I emphasize that you must lay the groundwork with your administration and the parents, but you will be very pleased with the results.

TIP: When I shared this with a group in Florida, an assistant principal told me that when he was teaching, he did something similar, but he didn't let his kids make below a B because he felt average wasn't good enough. I agree; most of our kids can do better than average if given the opportunity and instruction. Imagine your kids' reactions when you tell them they will all earn only As and Bs next grading period. That is a high expectation.

"Average is as close to the bottom as it is to the top."
—Anonymous

TEAM
(Together Everyone Achieves More)
Develops cooperation, trust, integrity, responsibility, caring

This is a technique I learned about recently. I implemented it for one semester only, in one class, and enjoyed it greatly. The idea came to me from "Boom Boom" Jackson, an educational coach and motivator from Houston, Texas, where he runs a K-8 private school. In a presentation, he discussed the TEAM procedure. It sounded good, so I gave it a try the next week with my freshman civics class, which consisted of 25 mixed-ability and mixed-behavior children. It worked great!

Students were placed in groups of three or four as a team and told to come up with a team name, logo, banner, and slogan. The students on each team sat together and were told that as a team they were responsible for their own work and the group's work—all for one and one for all. They had to help teammates get assignments when they were out, review for quizzes and tests, etc. Peer pressure was at work here: If one person on the team forgot homework or didn't do a class assignment, they all had to do it over! They generally didn't do most work together, yet the success of each depended on the completed work of their teammates. They didn't all receive the same grade, but team averages were calculated once a month, with the highest team average winning a candy bar or some similar small prize. At the end of the semester, I told them I would take the team with the highest average out to dinner at the restaurant of its choice. (The "Hotdogs" chose Outback!)

Another key component of this was even higher expectations than A-B-C-Incomplete. Under the TEAM concept, no one could make below a 100! If they did, the whole team had to make up the test or quiz or assignment. This sounded tough, but with extra-credit questions thrown in and study groups available, it worked well. The kids worried a little about the amount of work this would mean, but they also loved the idea of a guaranteed A. Going out to dinner at the end of the year was a good incentive as well. Each team was very competitive.

Now, some of the kinks: I had one student who didn't want to join a team. He wanted to be on his own. I didn't force him. He worked alone, doing his own banner and slogan. I also had about three kids who were in class very rarely (50 out of 180 days) and often in jail. I had started them out in teams, and they loved the idea, but outside factors kept them from being good teammates, so we agreed to drop them from teams. I also fudged a little on the 100 for every assignment. I never relaxed on tests or quizzes, but on some worksheets or homework assignments I may not have made them all do it over if only one person missed a question or two. Also, there were a couple times when a team member didn't get in to retake a test or quiz, causing his team's average to go down.

The results were tremendous. In a comparison of quarter grades, before and after TEAM was implemented, the grade results were as follows:

BEFORE:	As-4	Bs-9	Cs-7	Ds-3	Fs-2
AFTER:	As-18	Bs-4	Cs-3	Ds-0	Fs-0

My kids were amazed and proud. They had worked hard and together to earn this success. I was proud of them. TEAM helped out in many ways. Not only did these kids lift their class grades up, but they also did very well on the N.C. end-of-course exam. Keep in mind this was a class with nearly two dozen IEPs, EC children, and numerous at-risk referrals. They proved something here!

TIP: You might want to try phasing in the TEAM concept one component at a time. I've had some teachers tell me they try something similar, and with great success, but just with homework. Others have said they only do it with quizzes and writing assignments. Phasing it in one section or area at a time might make the total concept stronger by semester's end. This practice leaves room for plenty of adaptations to your class.

"A great flame follows a little spark."

—Dante

Procedures and Their Practice
Develops responsibility

This is something I learned from Harry Wong and Phil Vincent, something that every elementary teacher knows and probably does. Children will do what they are repeatedly led and encouraged to do. That principle does not change when they get out of the fifth grade, but we secondary teachers have forgotten it. Coaches, on the other hand, hopefully live by it—practice, practice, practice, with the goals of getting better and gaining consistency.

A procedure is the steps that are taken to perform an action. In schools we often practice the procedure for fire drills, tornado drills and the like, so why don't we establish procedures for daily student activities and practice them? In my classroom I like my students to know procedures for handing in papers, tests, and homework; coming into class and getting to work; giving me admit slips when they have been absent; leaving class; taking notes; and asking questions. I know how I want these things to be done, the way that will be most orderly and efficient for my classroom. It is my responsibility to convey to my kids how I expect these things done. It is also my responsibility to make sure we practice those things that need practice.

At the beginning of each school year, I take probably fifteen minutes per period that first week to practice the procedures that I want my students to do that year. For example, in a high school classroom, the way students enter class and what they do to prepare to work is tremendously important to the success of that class that day. I instruct and demonstrate to my students the procedure I want them to follow when they come in the class each day. Then I take them all outside in the hallway, bookbags and all, and instruct them to go into the class using my procedures. We will usually do this three or four times, until everyone gets it right. Teachers and students who walk by just smile because they know what I'm doing with thirty kids in the hallway.

I know some folks will say that this is a waste of valuable time, especially when we have so much to cover in so little time. I disagree. My belief, and what I have seen to be true, is that this practice will save me hours down the road. My students know what is expected, and they practice the procedure until it's a habit. I now have MORE time on task. If I ever feel that we're getting a bit slack with the proper procedure, we practice it again. I generally have to do this after winter break and spring break. Here are the benefits to my classroom: the development of responsibility, organization, more time for teaching and discussions, and a stable routine, which all children need. Could you use any of those? It also makes my job easier, not having to yell all the time and looking around to find things. No teacher should live without procedures and their practice.

TIP: This is easy to expand and should be expanded past your classroom. Other great places to set and practice procedures include the media center and for any and all assemblies. So many school nowadays shy away from assemblies and the old "pep rally" because they say kids don't know how to behave. Well, we can't assume anything. If we want them to act one way or another, we have to show them how and practice the correct way.

"Practice makes perfect."

Seating Charts
Develops cooperation, community

Nell Ridge substituted at my high school for more than fifteen years. She was in her early 80s when she passed away last year. Mrs. Ridge often had a hard time with some of the classes she covered at our school, but I was very pleased when she told me that she always enjoyed covering my classes because my lessons were organized and I had seating charts. I said I thought everyone had seating charts, but she informed me otherwise—she had found that fewer teachers used seating charts than those who didn't. I was astonished because they had always been such an important tool for me.

Seating charts can be used so many ways. Obviously they help at the start of the year so I can learn names and faces. With 140-170 kids per day, I need all the help I can get in remembering their names. I know that middle school and high school students do not like assigned seats. They gripe for two minutes straight, but once I tell them that's the way it is, they're fine the rest of the year.

Once I've learned names and learned what kids not to place next to their friends, I change seating charts almost monthly. When I change seat assignments, I strategically place kids where I want them or where they best need to be. I don't put all the "bad" kids, or kids who are failing, up front. I don't want to use the seating chart to stigmatize anyone. I try to make sure that I don't place a child who has difficulty paying attention next to a window or near many friends, but I do want my kids to feel relaxed and have someone nearby with whom they feel comfortable.

I don't mind if two friends are next to each other, as long as they are able to keep quiet and do their work. If a student who teachers would normally place up front to keep him on task wants to sit in the back, I give him that opportunity as long as he is productive. It almost becomes an award system.

I personally like to keep my seats in straight rows. Harry Wong reports research that shows children do better in that type seating arrangement. I've tried other ways, but for me to be able to move around the room comfortably and give everyone a hand when they need it, or a pat on the back, the straight rows work best for me. We sometimes move our seating for a period based on what we are doing that day.

Seating charts are also a great way to build community in the classroom and to place people near good peer role models. Besides, they help out substitutes a lot, too.

TIP: If you change your seating charts often, as I do, it might be good to create a blank on an overhead sheet and fill it in every time you change. That way when kids come to class they can look up on the screen and see where they are supposed to sit. This can save a lot of time and debate. Change seats fairly often to keep the mix of your students fresh.

> "When I approach a child, he inspires in me two sentiments: tenderness for what he is and respect for what he may become."
>
> —Louis Pasteur

Day One Letter
Develops connection, respect, responsibility, integrity

My guess is that every teacher in America—and possibly around the world for that matter—has some form of letter he or she hands out on the first day of school. The purpose of these letters is usually to present the class and school rules, tell what the kids need to bring to class, and sometimes give an idea of what will be covered throughout the year. This is fine, but I think so much more can be done.

The paperwork you give to the students the first day, and ultimately send home to the parents, is a large part of that first impression you give to students and parents. In making that first impression, particularly with parents, I think it's vital to come across as a top-notch teacher and professional, well organized, disciplined, and one with high expectations for all of his or her students. All parents want their children to have the very best teacher possible. It is your duty to let them know that is exactly what they have gotten. If those parents are to be your allies for the next 180 days, you need to get off on the right foot. Remember that your first impression with the students may be great because they get to meet you, see you and hear you talk, get a feel for your personality, and they probably know your reputation. Parents usually don't have that opportunity. Your letter, syllabus, folder—whatever—will do that for you.

Students also read that first day's paperwork so they can get an idea about you and the class. They are smart and need to have the same strong message conveyed to them that you send to the parents. Students need to see and hear that you are going to be firm and fair, demanding and caring, and that your expectations are high for them all.

I have included some ideas I use in my Day One Letter. I keep this on my computer because inevitably I alter something every year, as I learn more. Over the years I have asked dozens of my teacher friends if I could have a copy of what they send home that first day. I'm always trying to get good ideas and become more efficient, and my colleagues' help has been invaluable. Following are tips for writing your own strong, positive Day One letter. I'm always looking for others' ideas.

- I use a print size that will get it all on one page. I don't like to hand out so many papers that they get lost in the pile, or that the significance is lost.

- I make this letter my students' first homework assignment. They are to sign it and have a parent or guardian sign it and bring it back to me the next day. The signatures signify that this is a contract between all three parties involved in that child's education. You might want to give a copy of the signed letter to the student.

- From day one I want my kids and their parents to know what this class is all about—student success. I describe the high expectations I set for my students. I don't want there to be any surprises for anyone involved.

- I try to place great emphasis on the responsibility that both my students and I have. I also want to show rewards.

- In my classroom, rule/guideline number one is RESPECT All Others in the Classroom, but I need to explain it. It's a general guideline, and different people view respect differently. What is a sign of respect to me may not mean the same thing to my students or their parents. Describe it in your letter, and repeat it during the first class day, along with the rundown of your class rules. Make sure all the kids know what your expectations are regarding respect.

- I write out all my classroom policies. If I put it on paper, I do my best to enforce it.

- I mention that I almost never give homework on Fridays. Obviously large reports, exams, and other unusual circumstances may require that work be done on the weekend, but I don't like giving homework on the weekends. Why? The golden rule—I don't like doing school work on the weekend if I can help it. That time is for my family and home obligations. Our students often have the same or similar weekend responsibilities. Students really appreciate this show of respect. This makes it more palatable for them to do the homework during the week.

- I write to stay positive and enthusiastic. I don't want my letter to intimidate or instill fear in my kids.

I think this Day One Letter has paid great dividends for me. In the past eleven years, I've had virtually zero parent complaints. When parents see the opportunities and high, positive expectations that I have for their children, they get behind me 100%. My students also realize that they have every opportunity to succeed, and that if they don't, they can only blame themselves. It takes away the excuses.

TIP: Many teachers I know use a complete syllabus when giving handouts on that first day. I love this idea because it lays everything on the table for students and their parents. Many high school kids hear the word syllabus and think of college. That's fine, because they now have a buffed-up image of your class and expectations.

"It's easy to make a buck. It's a lot tougher to make a difference."

—Tom Brokaw

Quote of the Week
Develops overall character and connection

I owe my friend and fellow teacher/coach Steve Bare for this idea. Steve picked it up from his senior English teacher, Mrs. Tormey, who used it effectively. I know that many other teachers use this; some do it daily and some monthly. What I do here is put a thought-provoking, meaningful quote up at the top of my chalkboard at the start of each week. My kids are responsible for copying it and reflecting on it at some point in the week. It makes them think about things and gives them an opportunity to talk about issues outside the textbook. The quote of the week is often great for a short discussion, writing assignment, critical-thinking piece, or just nice to read. Since my students have these quotes in their notebooks, it's very common for them to hear about something in the news or study about something in class and then come back and relate it to a past quote. Several are so powerful that I hold them responsible for knowing the quote and who said it for the rest of the year. A good example is Margaret Thatcher's "Freedom does not include the freedom from responsibility."

Sprinkled throughout this book are some of my favorite Quotes of the Week for you to use. They are easy to find at any bookstore or library, or on the Internet. It's neat when your students get hooked on them and start bringing in their favorites to share with you. I can be sure that if I forget to put up a new quote for the week, it won't be long before my kids are asking for one.

TIP: I've seen two great adaptations to this practice. One is to have your kids keep a separate quote journal, relating the given quote to their own lives, plus an in-depth analysis. Many kids will keep their quote journal forever. Another great idea is to have the kids use their quotes as a homework assignment that they are to share and discuss with their parents.

"Some people see things and say 'Why?' I see things and say 'Why not?'"

—Robert Kennedy

ABO Bucks
Develops connection, climate, respect, responsibility, caring

An ABO buck—so-called for my nickname of Coach Abo (short for Abourjilie)—is simply an enlarged copy of a dollar bill, front side only, with your picture in the place of George Washington's. I printed mine on green paper. I know it seems silly, but kids love it, and it works. I actually got this idea at an Advanced Placement workshop several years ago when I was teaching AP U.S. history. An ABO buck is similar to a homework pass that many teachers use. The concept is to reward students for doing something good—getting started quickly, giving a great answer to a question presented in class, or even helping others.

When the kids see your picture on your "buck" they will laugh and think you've gone crazy. That's okay, though. A little fun never hurt anyone. That alone will help the atmosphere of your classroom. I give ABO bucks to students for some behavior, act, or answer that was really good. The value of the buck is that they can later be traded in for credit on assignments.:

ABO Buck Trade-in Policy

5 = a free 100 on a homework or class assignment, or a pop quiz
7 = a free 100 on a quiz
17 = a free 100 on any test!!

I have a lot of fun with this, and kids love the idea of getting something for free, but they really don't. I don't give ABO bucks out for nothing. Kids earn them, and they usually don't know when I've got them on me to give out.

This is a great way to get everyone involved with a reward system and make kids realize that they have earned a reward. My students know I don't give them out every day but that I always have them ready to reward outstanding effort, kindness, or citizenship.

I also am able to differentiate the reward to the ability level of the student. Students classified as exceptional for one reason or another love the feeling of success and satisfaction that earning ABO bucks gives. I have used these at all class ability levels, and with all grades. Using ABO bucks is a great way to spice up test or unit reviews.

Students can keep their bucks for the entire year or cash them in at any time. At the end of the semester I will hold an ABO buck cash-in day when kids with fewer than five can turn theirs in for a few points on assignments. This way everybody can earn some credit with their bucks.

The only problem that I've had to nip in the bud at times is someone taking someone else's bucks. If that becomes an issue, you can always do away with ABO bucks for that class or write the name of the recipient on the bucks as you hand them out. The first year I did this, some of my freshman started offering their friends money for the bucks, but that was stopped quickly and has never been an issue since.

ABO bucks are a great way to increase student participation, motivation, and ultimately achievement. They're a lot of fun, too.

TIP: Another way to have fun and increase students' participation and motivation is to use a "thinking ball." I use a small, soft, squishy ball. When I'm asking questions, I tell my kids they must have the ball in their hands to answer, and we toss it around as needed. Not only does it allow students more response time, but it holds their attention and keeps 'em on their toes.

"Fortune favors the bold."

—Virgil

My House
Develops connection, respect, caring   ·

This is one of many great ideas that I got from Clare Lemeres several years ago. It was an immediate hit with both my students and me. I have used it ever since and will as long as I teach. This activity is one that will usually take up one entire class period. I know that sounds like a lot of time, but actually it is a great investment toward the climate and atmosphere of your classroom. I usually do this sometime around the fifth to seventh week of school, after completing a large unit of study. It's a great activity for a Friday when you don't want to launch into a new unit.

The way I do this activity is to have my kids get into groups of four with their desks together in a small circle, all facing each other. Their desks are cleared except for a pen or pencil. Then I hand out a sheet with a line drawing of a house on it.

I also show the same drawing on the overhead projector that I work on while they are doing theirs. We do it together. I ask my kids to draw a small picture in each part of the house as I describe what is to go in each section. It's not important that you or your kids be great artists. That is half the fun, looking at everyone's stick people. I ask them to keep what they are drawing to themselves. We will all share our houses with our group when we are finished.

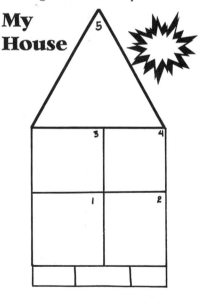

Here's what I ask them to put in each room:

Room #1: Most significant event in their life, from birth to present. (This doesn't have to be something positive. You may get divorces or deaths, as well as graduations and births. They can draw two if they can't choose just one.)

Room #2: Greatest accomplishment within the last 2-3 years.

Room #3: Something that they do well (sport, reading, being a friend, shopping, talking on the phone, etc.). You may have to remind older kids to keep it clean! There will be plenty of goofy smirks.

Room #4: Something that they know a lot about. (This may be the same thing as in #3, but that's okay.)

Room #5: What they would like to do or become if they were assured of success with no chance of failure. If it was guaranteed, what dream or goal would they want to see come true.

Foundation/3 Steps at the bottom: In each step write one word that describes your personality or character.

After they have completed their houses, it is time to share. I always start, sharing mine on the overhead with the entire class. This way, my kids get to know me a little better—it's another way to build our relationship. Once I'm done, I tell my kids to share with their group of four, one person speaking at a time and displaying a drawing. I walk around and listen to all the groups. What a lot of important things we learn about each other! Kids learn they're not alone in certain situations and feelings, and they may try harder to be friends with someone they didn't know well. All too often kids go through five, ten or more years of school with many other kids, but really only know a few. This changes things and helps the kids make connections, bringing them a little closer to each other and me.

I am always amazed how my students, 14-18 years old, like to tell others about themselves. The first time I did this I remember Steven coming up to me to show me his house. He asked if he could tape it to the chalkboard for everyone to see. Within five minutes I had more than 30 "houses" on my chalkboard. By the end of the day I had more than 100 covering half a wall. It was great. Have your kids sign their names above their houses so everyone will know whose they are.

TIP: Teachers from every grade, K-12, have told me that they love this activity and have been able to adapt it to their classes. One adaptation is to change the things that you want drawn in each room. A similar activity that I have used is one called "My Board of Directors." Here I tell my kids what a board of directors is and does, then have them identify those people in their lives who serve as their board of directors—who are their leaders, advisors and planners? Their role models and heroes? This is a great activity to discuss what a role model and/or hero is, and what virtues we admire in people. It's a great time to explain the difference between celebrity and role model to our students.

> "The actions of men are the best interpreters of their thoughts."
>
> —John Locke

Bits of Teaching Wisdom That I've Seen Work
Develops connection, climate, respect, caring

Don't stay behind a desk

I think we all know this, but we don't all do it. We heard it in college. We heard it in first-year training. Yet we remember what we saw modeled during our last four or five years of college: professors lecturing from behind a podium, desk, or lab table. Did you ever have you attention wander in such a class? Being on your feet for six-plus hours walking around during the school day gets tiring—very tiring. We may sit one day for a break, but it's too easy to get attached to a desk or chair. What's easy isn't best for our students.

Children need the interaction and personal guidance that a moving-and-touching teacher can give. So many of our kids feel there are barriers between us and them that we need to make an effort to break down that barrier, to close that distance. As I walk around a classroom I can monitor what each student is doing. Are they on task? I can make sure they're doing their own work. I can stop and whisper a word of encouragement or help to guide a student in need. Moving around the classroom, spreading my attention to all my children, has helped the overall atmosphere. I know who struggles and who might need a little extra help but won't go out of their way to ask for it. It also helps keep order. It's harder to act up when the teacher is talking from the back of the room.

Almost every time I've had problems in my class—kids looking for answers from other kids, students mouthing off to each other, etc.—was when I was sitting at the front of the class and not up and moving. I've heard many teachers complain about disruptive kids, or not being able to control cheating or continual talking. When I walk by their rooms, I always see them trying to teach from behind a desk. Don't get me wrong, there are plenty of times when I am at my desk—while my students are doing a class assignment, or when I'm working with a student at that time—but I try to move around as much as possible. Getting out from behind that desk doesn't sound like a big deal, but little things can have the greatest impact.

Service Learning

I am a firm believer in Martin Luther King, Jr.'s words, "All men can be great, because all men can serve." I have never done more than classroom service learning projects—yet I have seen those make a difference. There are many schools around the country doing wonders with service learning. One of the finest models anywhere is at Ferndale Middle School in High Point, North Carolina. Their program, P.R.I.D.E., has raised more than $17,000 in the last five years to give to their local Urban Ministries shelter. They have also worked on numerous Habitat for Humanity homes and other projects, most notably raising money for and awareness of Iodine

Deficiency Disorder. The project's coordinator, Vickie Miller, says it all started when her class decided to pick up pennies tossed away on the floor. Now, more than 500 children, grades six through eight, participate in P.R.I.D.E. Ferndale is an inner-city school made up of a diverse population with a large number of its children on free and reduced lunch. Since 1995, Ferndale has seen a gradual and definite increase in academic achievement and a significant decrease in disciplinary problems. Children are being given responsibility, a chance to help and encourage others, and are thriving!

If your school has a service learning program in place, encourage your classes to be leaders in the school. If not, develop your own projects. Within my classes, I have often given my kids service requirements that consist of hours served helping others. There are always initial groans, but once the kids start their service, they begin asking when they get to go again. Finding work for your class to do is easy—just call local retirement homes, churches, children's hospitals and the like. There have been many times when I've taken my freshman classes, one class at a time, to help our school janitor clean up the cafeteria and hallways after lunch. This helps instill in the kids that they have a responsibility to keep our school clean. It's also nice to help Mr. Carter with a big mess. My kids also enjoy going to help with middle and elementary school students. Several of my students have enjoyed helping the students in our special education (EMH, TMH/Life skills) class.

Whether you take on a large schoolwide project, such as the one at Ferndale Middle, or you just do things within your own class, service learning is a terrific component for any classroom. No time spent helping others is ever wasted, and the lessons learned by your students will be lasting and meaningful.

Jump Start

I don't believe there's a rule that says you can't start class until the bell rings. I learned that by watching two of my teacher friends get their kids started as soon as they walked through the classroom door. Richard Welch and Terri Green are not only friends but also master teachers. For years, I was amazed at how their kids got to work as soon as they hit the door. I wanted my classes to do that some time. The key was the expectations of the teacher. Richard handed his calculus students papers, tests, quizzes as soon as they walked in the class. He met them at the door, work in hand. In Terri's class, the kids knew that the split second the bell rang they would be under way with a Latin assignment. Richard and Terri are recognized as two of the greatest teachers ever in our school, but they're also recognized as two of the most caring. They are demanding and always get the best out of their kids. Their students love them.

I have found that my daily assignment helps me create the same type of atmosphere at times. If I want to make sure my kids are getting that early start, before the bell rings to begin class, I will often hand them a pop quiz, quiz or test right after I shake their hands at the doorway. You will find that the kids will groan and look at you like you are crazy at first, but within seconds they will be at work. I don't do this on a daily basis, but it keeps my kids on their toes, builds responsibility, and sets the level of expectations.

"Hey You!"

Learn the names of your students as soon as you possibly can. I try to have my seating chart ready within the first three days of school. I need this to learn their names. My students need it so that they don't feel like some stranger in a room that they will be in for the rest of the year. There is no sound more pleasing to a child than to hear his or her name called in a pleasant manner. Even to call students down for something, it is best to use their names. Using a student's name—as opposed to "Hey, you"—is the basis for building that relationship. When you call a child by name, especially in a school with several hundred to more than a thousand students, your remembering his or her name makes a big difference to a child. They realize you care. It may not seem like much, and it make take some real effort on your part in the first few days of school, but your students will tell you that it means a great deal to them.

No Excuses

I don't take time to listen to too many excuses from students. If you've been teaching for any amount of time, you have already heard every excuse in the book, and some are amazing. I know I have, so I tell my kids that I don't want excuses—I just want them to do what they need to do, as soon as they can. I'm not talking about cases of prolonged illness or family emergencies here. I mean the daily little things. In my class, the bottom line is, Have you done the required work? I'll accept some work late because situations do come up where work can't be done on time. I wish I always had my work done right on time and papers handed back the next day, but there are times that I don't. When kids hand in late work, they know that points will be deducted but that I will accept it. By accepting no excuses, just the work, I don't let students off the hook by simply giving them a zero. I want them to learn and work. Building that responsibility is priority one. I use other times and methods to work on punctuality.

I think what keeps the majority of my kids up to date with their work is knowing that the work keeps on coming. If you get behind on one task, the next will be on the way soon. They don't want to get in a hole. On the wall in my room hangs a large banner with a saying that I heard Marva Collins uses with her students—"Results and Responsibility—Not Excuses." This policy guides my classes.

No Red Ink

Another policy that I credit to Clare Lemeres, and I believe she said she got it from Marva Collins, is not to use red ink when I grade papers. This one is purely psychological, but the kids notice it right away.

Red often symbolizes negative things such as blood, death, "Red Scare," and academic failure. What do kids think when they get a paper back and the first thing they see are red marks and x's all over the paper? We teachers, from kindergarten to twelfth grade, have conditioned them to look for the red. To them it means failure. So, all I try to do is use another color—blue, black, green, purple, or pencil. The last feeling that I want my students to have when they get a test or any assignment back is fear of failure. What I choose to grade with can affect my kids psychologically.

Have Fun...and Don't Always Be So Quiet

If you aren't having fun teaching, you might be in the wrong business. If your students don't sometimes have fun and laugh in your class, they and you are missing out. This is a tough job we've chosen, with great demands, many challenges, hundreds of decisions to make daily, and the relentless drumbeat to get through the curriculum. I think the same goes for our kids. It's not always easy being a student, child, or teenager today. We owe it to ourselves and our kids to laugh a little and have some fun in class.

Our students are funny. Laugh with them. Funny things happen in class. Don't be afraid to smile. Way too many people in the education business think that you have to be stern and hard on the kids the first few weeks of school to set the tone and that you can loosen up later. That's crazy! The tone you set by never smiling or showing your kind and funny side is that "this class is not going to be enjoyable and I don't care about you personally. I will show no emotion. My job is to teach. Your job is to learn." I think we can set high expectations and demands on our students, and at the same time show them why we got into education in the first place—because we care about children and want to help them learn and make the most of their lives. Students respect and appreciate that. They'll learn in your class and want to be there. James Hind was right on target when he said, "Students want to know how much you care before they care how much you know."

Hal Urban has his students share something funny weekly. What a great practice. Hal knows that people feel better, both physically and mentally, when they laugh. He tries to start each day off on a positive note. I don't do any special humor assignments like Hal does, but I do always take time to laugh at the funny things in class or share funny things with my kids. (I also tell funny stories about myself—kids love to know that you are human.) If you do that they too will share their funny stories and jokes. You will notice an improvement in your classroom climate and in the relationships you form with your students.

Along that same line, we need to debunk the myth that a good classroom is a silent classroom. I disagree completely. Learning isn't always a silent process. I want my kids to question and explore. I want them to discuss ideas and challenge thoughts they may have had previously. Children need to interact and share ideas. Sometimes it can get downright loud, but I want them active and involved. In industry, people talk about the roar or buzz of productivity. I think that same principle can, at times, apply to the classroom. If they are too quiet, be careful—they might be asleep.

Laugh, learn, smile, cry, hug, love...TEACH with a passion!

"I touch the future. I teach."

—Christa McAuliffe

Closing Thoughts

Thank you for taking your time to read some or all of what is in this book. These are just some of the things I have learned during my time as a teacher. I borrowed most of these ideas from great teachers, tweaked them to fit my classes, and next thing you know...my class was transformed. Not every day at school is the greatest in the world, but I always look forward to the next. The relationships I build with my students are the most satisfying part of the work.

Don't let anyone tell you, and don't you ever believe, that you can't teach a certain group of children or that they can't learn from you or respect you because you aren't the right color, sex, or size. That is hogwash. Many years ago I heard a man say that the biggest problem in our district was that "white teachers can't teach black students." I just grinned and thought to myself, "This man has no idea." It doesn't matter what color my students are, how well they speak the English language, what size house they live in, or what level of school their parents completed. Those may be factors in their lives, but they have never stopped my students from learning in my class. What matters is why I'm there in the classroom and why they are there at school. We may not even be there for the same reasons, but that can change. What matters is my attitude.

I don't treat every student the same. They're not all the same, and I try to give each of them what they need. For some it may be a hug, for others a stern rebuke. It might be extended time on a test or assignment, preferential seating, or a sympathetic ear after class. Regardless of the differences among them, or between them and me, I want to provide them all with a strong, caring role model and the best possible education that I can provide. If you take that as your mission, you will love teaching and your children as much as I do.

Thank you for choosing to teach. It is the greatest opportunity in the world. Good luck and have fun!

"Children want to know how much you care before they care how much you know."

—James Hind

AFTERWORD
Ten More Good Reasons for Character Education

In Dr. Thomas Lickona's *Educating for Character: How Our School Can Teach Respect and Responsibility,* he identified ten wide-ranging reasons for the need for character education, not only in our schools but within our society. His splendid work appeals to all of us—parents, educators, neighbors, and community leaders. Lickona identified the following reasons:

1. The dire and urgent need is evident in the statistics of how children are hurting themselves in today's society.

2. Transmitting values is and always has been the work of civilization.

3. The school's role as moral educator is at a premium as children are receiving less and less personal attention at home.

4. There is common ethical ground, even in our own value-conflicted society.

5. Democracies have a special need for moral education because democracy is a government by the people themselves.

6. There is no such thing as a value-free education.

7. The great questions facing both the individual person and the human race are moral questions.

8. There is a broad-based, growing support for character education in the schools.

9. An unabashed commitment to moral education is essential if we are to attract and keep good teachers.

10. Character education is a doable job.

I can't improve on this list. I use it daily as I work with character education and speak to civic and parent groups, teachers, and administrators. Yet in our era of tremendous outside pressure on teachers to focus primarily on test scores, I feel there is a need to give teachers and schools some other, more directly focused reasons for them to embrace and adopt character education. That is why I call this list "10 More Reasons for Character Education."

1. Purpose. Anyone involved in education, whether as a teacher, administrator, PTA officer, or superintendent, got into education to touch the lives of children. We all wanted to somehow inspire and improve the lives of young people. No teacher got into teaching to be the national testing service, or for the great pay, or the long (and shrinking) summers. Forming relationships with children, showing children the right way to go—this is character development, and this is why we got into teaching in the first place. We all wanted to, and still want to, make a difference.

2. Transition. Across the country there is often great discussion about transition programs—how to make the transition from elementary school to middle school, and from middle school to high school. These truly are challenging times for our students and teachers. Character education is the ideal "transition program" because, when character education is created and treated as a K-12 process, transition becomes easy for children. A common set of virtues and values are present in both schools. What develops are common language and common expectations for behavior. When there is a unity between the schools, the transition for the children, parents, and teachers becomes much easier.

3. Diversity. As our schools and country head into the next millennium, our communities, hallways, and classrooms are more diverse than ever. There are continual questions about what to do concerning multicultural education. One of the first tasks is finding a common ground among us all. Once we can do that, true respect and appreciation for others can take place. One central tenet that we all hold dear is what many call the Golden Rule. In Judaism it is stated as "What you hate, do not do to anyone." In Islam it is "No one of you is a believer until he loves for his brother what he loves for himself." A Yoruba Proverb from Nigeria says, "One going to take a pointed stick to pinch a baby bird should first try it on himself to feel how it hurts." (For a longer list see the Appendix). We all seem to have in common this underlying tenet and desire of respect for self and others. This is found in all faiths and in all cultures. All of us, no matter our race, religion, or socioeconomic status, want our children to be respected and be respectful of others. We want our children to be good people. We just don't all always know how to develop this in our children. This common desire can be a starting place for diverse communities to come together for a better future. You can't have a successful, meaningful cultural diversity program if the issue of character and respect for all isn't addressed in the beginning.

4. Workforce readiness. There is a great call upon today's schools to ready our children for the work world. Much of this preparation focuses upon both technical and vocational education. Without a doubt, there is a tremendous need for these avenues to be traveled. At the same time, we must not fail to give employers the character attributes that they are crying for from their employees: honesty, reliability, responsibility, respect for self and others, caring, and determination. Ninety-five percent of individuals who lose their first job do so not because they are incapable of performing the job, but rather over an issue of character. In the words of business leader Barnaby C. Keeney: "At college age, you can tell who is best at going to school and taking tests, but you can't tell who the best people are. And that worries the hell out of me."

5. Focus. With all of the societal and bureaucratic pressures on teachers in our public schools today, it's easy for teachers to lose sight of why they are there. All too often we are bombarded by test-score statistics, threats of school violence, threats of lawsuits if an error is made, the demands to improve our numbers and close the gaps, and questions about our competency and abilities from the media. Through it all, too few people remember that teachers are in the people business. We are there for children, not solely for test scores and always shading the correct bubble. Students require much more than a sharpened No. 2 pencil and practice tests to be successful in life. Teachers know this and that is why we are here. We cannot afford to lose our focus. Our students cannot afford for us to lose our focus. Character education and that focus on the child will help us to regain our focus as professional educators.

6. NOT the "Flavor of the Month." Educating for character is not a new program. It is a process—a deliberate process that is as old as public education in our country itself. Up until the 1960s, public schools in America adhered strongly to the call for civility and citizenship. Schools and teachers were there to produce not just test takers, but rather good citizens, good people. Through the tumultuous '60s and '70s our schools lost sight of that focus. Slowly, since the mid-1980s, educators have started to realize what we lost and have worked to get it back. Now we are facing the opportunity to seize our schools and children back. Programs don't work. Processes centered on serving children and society do work. Character education is nothing new, rather simply reemerging as an integral need that too many have lost sight of.

7. "At-Risk" students. For far too long, schools and systems across the country have spent millions of dollars on programs targeting "at-risk" children. Most of these programs come in a box, a folder, or a video and really only serve as a Band-aid® that can only temporarily mask a deeper problem within too many of our children. Children need mentors, role models, and caring adults in their lives.

They crave nurturing, caring, positive relationships—the essence of character education. As the old saying goes, "You've got to reach 'em, before you can teach 'em." All children—and I mean ALL children—want to be successful and appreciated and to feel a sense of belonging. At one point or another in their lives, all children could be labeled "at-risk." These wonderful children simply need the direction and caring climate that we all can create.

8. Safe Schools. Did you ever notice that in all the recent, notorious cases of school violence, no one was asking afterward what the test scores were of those schools? The media and public always ask, What went wrong with the kids? Where were the parents? Why didn't someone know something? How could this happen here? All too often blame is thrown around or people call for metal detectors, school uniforms, and even gun-toting teachers and principals. Safe schools aren't about fancy programs, more money, or improved self-defense. They are about the people inside those buildings and the environment they create. The same can be said of character education. It's not about pretty posters and motivational quotes. It's about people caring about people.

9. Achievement. When teachers have more time to teach in a civil, respectful environment, and children feel safe, appreciated and respected—then real achievement and learning can take place. Teachers and schools must create a strong learning environment, and character education can help provide the tools to do so. It's not magic. It is simply the essence of teaching. The evidence is clear, from Albuquerque, New Mexico, to Dayton, Ohio, to Thomasville, North Carolina, and hundreds of places in between, academic achievement can be a powerful byproduct of successful character education.

10. Teachers and Students. Character education is a gift for both teachers and students. Teachers want to teach. We want to positively touch the lives of the children we come in contact with on a daily basis. Students want to feel accepted. They want limits, structure, and guidance. Character education can be those things for both teachers and students. For the teacher, improved classroom climate and student motivation make our jobs much easier. Numerous teachers around the country report being rejuvenated by the progress they have seen, thanks in large part to their efforts in character education. All students will tell you that the teachers who mean the most to them are the ones who care. Character education is a win-win situation for all involved!

APPENDIX
A Global View of the Golden Rule

African Traditional Religions: One going to take a pointed stick to pinch a baby bird should first try it on himself to feel how it hurts (Yoruba proverb—Nigeria)

Baha'i Faith: He should not wish for others that which he doth not wish for himself.

Buddhism: Hurt not others with that which pains thyself.

Christianity: Do unto others as you would have them do unto you, and love your neighbor as yourself.

Hinduism: Do nothing to thy neighbors which thou wouldst not have them do to thee.

Islam: No one of you is a believer until he loves for his brother what he loves for himself.

Jainism: A man should wander about treating all creatures as he himself would be treated.

Judaism: What you hate, do not do to anyone.

Sikh: As thou deemst thyself, so deem others.

Taoism: Regard your neighbor's gain as your own gain, and your neighbor's loss as your own loss.

Zoroastrianism: Whatever is disagreeable to yourself do not do unto others.

Confucius: What you do not want done to yourself, do not do to others.

Aristotle: We should behave to our friends as we wish our friends to behave to us.

SOURCES: Josephson Institute of Ethics, 1996, and Amy Enderle

It Matters To This One

As I walked along the seashore
This young boy greeted me.
He was tossing stranded starfish
Back to the deep blue sea.
I said, "Tell me why you bother,
Why waste your time this way?
There's a million stranded starfish...
Does it matter, anyway?"
And he said, "It matters to this one.
It deserves a chance to grow.
It matters to this one,
I can't save them all, you know.
But it matters to this one.
I'll return it to the sea.
It matters to this one,
And it matters to me."

—Author Unknown

Bibliography & Suggested Readings

Barksdale, Thomas. *It's All About You*. Edgewood, Md.: Duncan & Duncan Inc., 1997.

Brown, Deb Austin. *Lessons From The Rocking Chair*. Chapel Hill, N.C.: Character Development Publishing, 1997.

Comer, James P. *School Power*. New York: The Free Press, 1980.

Covey, Stephen R. *The 7 Habits of Highly Effective People*. New York: Simon and Schuster, 1987.

Dent, Harry. *Teaching Jack and Jill Right vs. Wrong in the Homes and Schools*, Columbia, S.C., 1996.

DeRoche, Edward and Mary Williams. *Educating Hearts and Minds*. Thousand Oaks, Calif.: Corwin Press, Inc., 1996.

Fenchuk, Gary W. *Timeless Wisdom*. Midlothian, Va.: Cake Eaters, Inc., 1994.

Hoffman, Judith and Anne Lee. (1997), *Character Education Workbook: For School Boards, Administrators and Community Leaders*. Chapel Hill, N.C.: Character Development Group, 1997.

Kilpatrick, William. *Why Johnny Can't Tell Right From Wrong*. New York: Simon and Schuster, 1992.

Lemeres, Clare. *The Winner's Circle: Yes, I Can! Self-Esteem Lessons for the Secondary Classroom*. Newport Beach, Calif.: LaMeres Lifestyles Unlimited, 1997.

LeGette, Helen R. *Parents, Kids & Character*. Chapel Hill, N.C.: Character Development Publishing, 1999.

Lickona, Thomas. *Educating For Character: How Our Schools Can Teach Respect and Responsibility*. New York: Bantam Books, 1991.

McClary, Clebe with Diane Barker. *Living Proof*. Pawleys Island, S.C., 1978.

Purkey, William Watson and John M. Novak. *Inviting School Success*. Belmont, Calif.: Wadsworth Publishing Co., 1996.

Ryan, Kevin and Karen E. Bohlin. *Building Character in Schools*. San Francisco, Calif.: Jossey-Bass Publishers, 1998.

Urban, Hal. *Life's Greatest Lessons: 20 Things I Want My Kids to Know*. Redwood City, Calif.: Great Lessons Press, 1992.

Vincent, Philip F. *Developing Character In Students, A Primer*, 2nd ed. Chapel Hill, N.C.: Character Development Publishing, 1999.

_____. *Rules & Procedures for Character Education*. Chapel Hill, N.C: Character Development Publishing, 1998.

Wong, Harry and Rosemary Wong. *The First Days of School*. Sunnyvale, Calif.: Harry Wong Publications, 1991.

About the Author

In September 1983, Charlie Abourjilie realized his calling to become a high school teacher. Professor James O'Brian was the messenger. As a student at J. Sergeant Reynolds Community College in Richmond, Virginia, Charlie was so inspired and turned on to learning by his history professor, Dr. O'Brian, that he knew what he wanted to do with his life—light that same fire in children.

Charlie graduated from Virginia Polytechnic Institute and State University (Virginia Tech) in 1988. While working at Bear Island Paper Mill in Ashland, Virginia, that summer, Charlie was asked to interview for a teaching and coaching job in Guilford County, North Carolina. He accepted the job and has called Greensboro home ever since. He has taught and coached at Southwest Guilford High School for twelve years. Currently out of the classroom, he is the Character Education Coordinator, as a Teacher on Special Assignment, for Guilford County Schools. He teaches social studies and coaches football and women's basketball. He believes the coaching and teaching enrich each other, making him better at both.

Charlie lives in Greensboro with his wife, Karen, his daughter, Jordan, and his sons, Cole and Austin.

A dynamic speaker, Charlie has made presentations to hundreds of groups across the country—parents, teachers, and both business and community leaders—about character education, teaching at-risk youth, diversity education, and parenting for character.

Character Development Publishing Order Form *(PHOTOCOPY AS NEEDED)*

TITLE	PRICE	QTY.	$ TOTAL
Advisor/Advisee Character Education LESSONS FOR TEACHERS AND COUNSELORS Sarah Sadlow, 8x11, 120 pages, softcover, ISBN 0-9653163-7-8	$24.95		
America's Pride & Promise Teacher's Kit RELEARNING THE MEANING OF THE PLEDGE OF ALLEGIANCE Rhonda Adams, CD, Sheet Music, Teacher's Guide	$39.95		
Building Character Schoolwide BUILDING A CARING COMMUNITY IN YOUR SCHOOL R. Bernardo, L. Frye, D. Smith, G. Foy, 8x11, 153 pages, softcover, ISBN 1-892056-10-0	$18.00		
Caring Messages 40 WEEKS OF DAILY DISCUSSION IDEAS ON CHARACTER Sharon L. Banas, 8x11", 56 loose leaf pages, ISBN 1-892056-12-7	$14.95		
Character Education (K-6 Year 1) John Heidel and Marion Lyman-Mersereau 8x11,176 pages, softcover, #IP 420-1	$19.95		
Character Education (K-6 Year 2) John Heidel and Marion Lyman-Mersereau 8x11,176 pages, softcover, #IP 420-2	$19.95		
Character Education (6-12 Year 1) John Heidel and Marion Lyman-Mersereau 8x11,176 pages, softcover, #IP 421-1	$19.95		
Character Education (6-12 Year 2) John Heidel and Marion Lyman-Mersereau 8x11,176 pages, softcover, #IP 421-2	$19.95		
Character Education Through Story LESSONS FROM MULTI-CULTURAL LITERATURE K-6 Dr. Joseph Hester, Paul Coble Fellow, 8x11, 488 pages, softcover, ISBN 1-892056-20-8	$39.95		
Cultivating Heart and Character T. Devine, J. H. Seuk, A. Wilson, 6x9, 486 pages, softcover, ISBN 1-892056-15-1	$22.95		
Developing Character for Classroom Success STRATEGIES FOR SECONDARY STUDENTS Charlie Abourjilie, 6x9, 96 pages, softcover, ISBN 1-892056-07-0	$12.00		
Developing Character in Students, 2nd Edition Dr. Philip Fitch Vincent, 6x9, 174 pages, softcover, ISBN 1-892-05604-6	$19.95		
Elementary School Guide to Character Education Steve Dixon, 6x9, 120 pages, softcover, ISBN 1-892056-17-8	$15.95		
A Gift of Character: The Chattanooga Story 6x9, 220 pages, softcover, ISBN 1-892056-16-x	$15.95		
Lessons From the Rocking Chair TIMELESS STORIES FOR TEACHING CHARACTER Deb Austin Brown, 6x9, 70 pages, softcover, ISBN 0-9653163-3-5	$8.95		
Life's Greatest Lessons 20 THINGS I WANT MY KIDS TO KNOW Hal Urban, 6x9, 162 pages, softcover, ISBN 0-9659684-4-8	$14.95		
Operating Manual for Character Education Programs 3-ring binder, 9x12, 327 pages, ISBN 1-892056-13-5	$79.95		
Parents, Kids & Character 21 STRATEGIES TO HELP YOUR CHILDREN DEVELOP GOOD CHARACTER Dr. Helen LeGette, 6x9, 180 pages, softcover, ISBN 1-892056-01-1	$15.95		
Rules & Procedures THE FIRST STEP TOWARD SCHOOL CIVILITY, 2ⁿᵈ EDITION Dr. Philip Fitch Vincent, 6x9, 96 pages, softcover, ISBN 1-892056-06-2	$14.00		
Rules & Procedures on Video THE FIRST STEP TOWARD SCHOOL CIVILITY (VIDEO) Dr. Philip Fitch Vincent, VHS, 44 minutes, ISBN 1-892056-03-8	$59.95		
Teaching Character...It's Elementary 36 WEEKS OF DAILY LESSONS FOR GRADES K-5 S. A. Broome, N. W. Henley, 8x11, 232 pages,softcover, ISBN 1-892056-08-9	$27.95		
Teaching Character: Parent's Idea Book A. C. Dotson and K. D. Wisont, 8x11, 84 pages, softcover, ISBN 0-9653163-5-1	$12.00		
Teaching Character: Teacher's Idea Book A. C. Dotson and K. D. Wisont, 8x11, 160 pages, softcover, ISBN 0-9653163-4-3	$24.00		

CHARACTER DEVELOPMENT PUBLISHING

Pay with credit card or make checks payable to:
Character Development Publishing
PO Box 9211, Chapel Hill, NC 27515
(919) 967-2110, (919) 967-2139 fax
Respect96@aol.com
www.CharacterEducation.com

Subtotal	
(North Carolina residents add 6.5%) Sales tax	
6% SHIPPING WITH A $4 MINIMUM Shipping	
TOTAL	

SHIP TO: Name _____

Organization _____ Title _____

Address _____

City _____ State: _____ Zip: _____

Phone: ( ) _____ Fax: ( ) _____ PO#: _____

Visa or MasterCard number: _____ Exp. Date: _____

Signature: _____

FAX your order
(919) 967-2139,
call us
(919) 967-2110,
or order from our website:
www.CharacterEducation.com

FAX your order (919) 967-2139